FIFTY-ONE MOVES

Ben Ashcroft

Fifty-One Moves
Ben Ashcroft

ISBN 978-1-904380-24-5 (Paperback)
ISBN 978-1-908162-48-9 (Adobe E-book)
ISBN 978-1-908162-49-6 (Kindle /Epub E-book)

Cover design © 2013 Waterside Press. Design by Verity Gibson/www.gibgob.com

Cataloguing-In-Publication Data A catalogue record for this book can be obtained from the British Library.

e-book *Fifty-One Moves* is available as an ebook and also to subscribers of Myilibrary, Dawsonera, Ebrary and Ebscohost.

Printed by Lightning Source, Milton Keynes.

Main UK distributor Gardners Books, 1 Whittle Drive, Eastbourne, East Sussex, BN23 6QH. Tel: +44 (0)1323 521777; sales@gardners.com; www.gardners.com

USA and Canada Ingram Book Company, One Ingram Blvd, La Vergne, TN 37086, USA. (800) 937-8000, orders@ingrambook.com, ipage.ingrambook.com

Published 2013 by
Waterside Press Ltd.
Sherfield Gables
Sherfield on Loddon
Hook, Hampshire
United Kingdom RG27 0JG

Telephone +44(0)1256 882250
E-mail enquiries@watersidepress.co.uk
Online catalogue WatersidePress.co.uk

Fifty-One Moves

Ben Ashcroft

Foreword by Dr Peter McParlin

WATERSIDE PRESS

Contents

Acknowledgements

I've had great support over the years off my close friends: Martin, Jay, Big Gaz, Damo, Graham, Gemma plus many more.

A very big thank you to those close friends who have helped me with my book: Damien Gravenor and Lisa Warwick.

Also special thanks to Amanda and Paul Robertson for all their help and hard work that I appreciate very much; and to Roger Harvey and Richard Harvey of Harveys Department Store in Halifax for their support, they have been amazing.

Becky Jennings has also been a massive support to me through everything (Like the Mom I didn't have).

My grateful thanks to Dr Peter McParlin for all his help, and kindly writing a short *Foreword*, he has been brilliant.

Also to Lisa Holmes; Richard Ian Smith; Kathleen Randall; Natalie Ashcroft and Gareth Schofield, who I owe a lot to for his support through all the bad times.

Ben Ashcroft
May 2013

About the author

Ben Ashcroft hails from Sowerby Bridge, West Yorkshire and from the age of ten spent his early life in the care of the local authority. Altogether, he was moved 51 times. When not "going missing" or "running away" he lived in a total of 37 different establishments and foster homes.

Like many young people with broken family ties, he ended up in a young offender institution. As an adult and after "sorting out his life", he has had a variety of mainly manual jobs and in his spare time began working with groups involved with young people in trouble, especially those from a similar background to his.[1] In 2012, he set out independently to motivate them, steer them away from crime, drugs and a destructive lifestyle and to inspire them with his message, "Never, ever give up!". He has since spoken to audiences large and small.

Ben's earnings from this book will be re-invested in this work, which is designed to reduce offending (or re-offending) and to give young people "the chance they deserve".

In his spare time, Ben enjoys fishing, walking, cycling and visiting some of his favourite places as described in the book.

---

1. Some of the bodies he has been associated with are mentioned in the final chapter. His contact details are: ben.ashcroft@51moves.org; Twitter: @AshcroftBen.

51Moves
Changing experiences

Ben now runs his own organization.
See **www.51moves.org** where you will find details of:

- Qualification training talks
- In service training talks
    - Services to facilitate participation/consultation with young people when undertaking reviews and reports
- Direct work with young people/offenders
    - Hard to reach young people/offenders through providing a positive role model/inspirational talks
    - 1-2-1 coaching service (different approach for young people in need).

His email is: **ben.ashcroft@51moves.org**

For Jack

Fifty-One Moves has been described as 'inspirational', 'powerful', 'emotional', 'compelling' and 'required reading' for anyone interested in the child care system. The following are examples of online reviews posted when the book was originally released in an embryonic Kindle version:

'An inspiring and moving account of the trauma and distress caused to a young boy by his family and our care system':

Sarah

'How do you fix pieces that have been utterly shattered–as a parent, ex-care man and professional psychologist I wish I knew–I guess the resolution to do so has to be out there':

Dr Peter MᶜParlin

'A very raw book…but this only adds to the sense of passion and honesty with which it is written':

Fiona Sorsby, Bingley, West Yorkshire

'This motivational read is such a hard hitting tale…it's heartfelt and gives such a clear first-hand account of life living in a care home…A brilliant worthwhile read about a man who truly turned his life around':

Stacey Spencer

Publishers note: Some names in the book have been changed.

Foreword

This book is brutal and reaches into our compassion. In fact it demands our compassion. Unlike the growing literature of severe abuse amongst our alleged "looked after" child population, it challenges the core concepts we have as members of society, or indeed as child care professionals. Simply, the number 51 indicts us all.

Ben's book conveys the unravelling of a childhood out-of-control; of parents and child care agencies totally self-absorbed and who have, fatefully, long since lost the plot.

Moreover and challengingly, it begs the question of how to put right such devastating and outmoded systems; that have led such a young boy, initially blameless, into such lamentable and appalling circumstances, into being locked away for most of his childhood.

What I can share with you as a reader of Ben's story is that the landscape of child care and custodial provision will change as a consequence of this book. The narrative is raw, asseverating and true. It forces us to reconsider the journey of childhood, where this childhood has been to, wreaked with havoc and fecklessness.

St Augustine of Hippo told us to separate the sinner from the sin and Ben's book clearly achieves that. It is not just a compelling true story but a tour de force for change within childcare.

Dr Peter McParlin
Fellow of the British Psychological Society

1   Life Before the Moves

My name is Ben, and this is my story. I live with my Mom Judy, and step-dad Terry, sister Natalie, and my dog Pippy. The dog was named after Pippy Longstocking, a fictional character from one of my favourite films when I was a young boy. I was a happy child, full of the joys of youth. At least I was at this point in my story.

One sunny Yorkshire morning I woke early, a nine-year-old lad readying myself for school. So I was up and dressed in my school uniform, I had my breakfast and brushed my teeth, then I made for my sister's bedroom. Natalie's room was next door to mine. "I'm ready!" I shouted enthusiastically, "ready for the day ahead."

It was a weekday so Natalie and I would walk the mile or so to school, the same walk we made every day together. We lived in a maisonette in Sowerby Bridge, West Yorkshire. The first thing a Yorkshire lad will tell anyone is that they're from Yorkshire, you won't even need to ask. That's how proud a Yorkshireman is of where he's from. Every Englishman feels a degree of pride about whichever part of the country he's from.

So we walk out of our front door up some stairs then through another door into the outside world. Outside our house there was a lush green grass bank which we used to play on, and at the top of the bank was the car park. My Mom wasn't working and didn't drive so we didn't have a car to park, which is why my sister and I always walked to school.

We proceeded up the bank, across the car park onto Hollins Lane which is a winding road leading to the bottom of Dixie Woods. Before you reached the woods there were some neglected buildings you had to pass to the left across open ground where there were some old, derelict factories. This led to the bridge where we crossed over the River Calder, passing by a football pitch and finally navigating our way through the woods. This would bring us up onto Sowerby New Road by the only sweet shop on the way to school. School was just down the road, where we would meet the little old lollipop lady. Every morning she would help us across the road and into school. I loved Sowerby New Road School—it's where I spent some of the best years of my life so far.

I look across the playground to try and spot any of my mates so I can go and meet them. The first person I see is my best friend Wayne Cartlidge, he has been my mate ever since I can remember. He's funny, mischievous, and cheeky—just like me.

We used to live next door to Wayne and his family. His parents were really strict and if I remember rightly there was his mum, dad and two brothers, Mark and Carl. Mark was ten-years-old—the same age as my sister—and Carl was a year or two younger than me and Wayne, we're nine-years-old. We're both football mad so that's all we did with our playtimes… played football, and after school we tried to get a kick about in as often as possible.

I go over to Wayne and he is with David, Robbie, and Ben. They're just about to start playing football. I go straight in goal, as I always did, and we play until the bell goes. We all loved football, including me. I only loved one thing more than school and football and that was fishing.

The bell goes so we go in sluggishly after collecting our bags and coats. We make our way in ready for class but don't do a lot that day, just some Maths and English and before you know it it's over. I wait for Natalie after school then we walk home the same way we had come, over the road and back through Dixie Woods, past the football pitches, then over the bridge with the River Calder flowing underneath it. Back past the old derelict buildings and up the winding road to the top that meets Hollins Lane, along Hollins Lane and right into the car park, then down the lush green banking back into the maisonettes, down the steps and finally into No.58 Marton Heights.

I get changed quickly and go outside into the woods at the side of Marton Heights. We used to climb trees and hang out off them and dare to see how high we could go, also in the woods we used to find newts and frogs. Just normal things kids do in such places. Best of all was Hill Top Dam, which was no more than 200-yards from our maisonette. I go fishing at Hill Top Dam before school, after school and at weekends too. If I'm not in school, or with Wayne, being cheeky to people: so we could get a chase off them, it is one of my favourite pastimes—you would always find me at the dam.

Me and Wayne would laugh and mess about if we were together, we were a pair of jokers really. We would go fishing together sometimes too, as we both liked similar things. We never did nothing—but we were always up to something.

So I'm approaching ten-years-old and I am with Wayne, Robbie and Roy all sat by the River Calder in Sowerby Bridge near to Wayne's family's flat. By the river are a few little weirs and canoe slaloms, and we are sat by the arch looking up to the main bridge in Sowerby Bridge. Wayne and me are sat behind Robbie and Roy on the big rocks that are on the banking next to the river. Robbie and Roy are cousins, both in my class at school. We are throwing stones into the river and messing about, but being the joker I am I look at Wayne and smile … I see the way he looks at me as if to say,

"*No way* are you going to push me in!"

"I *so am*," I'm thinking!

I lined up my feet with Roy's back and gave him a little shove into the river—not thinking for a second that he might hurt himself. He went face down with his hands out ready to stop himself, but the water was deeper than his arms, so he was going fully in anyway. You could hear the splash and then a groan from Roy. Wayne and I were in hysterics at the sight of Roy hitting the water.

Robbie helped Roy out, but we were still laughing hard! It wasn't until we looked at Roy and saw his wrist that we knew it was serious — it seemed dangerously deformed with a huge lump. We weren't laughing now, I was scared and didn't know what to do next. Roy was screaming out in dreadful pain and looking at his wrist. I couldn't blame him, it was in an awful state. I never meant to hurt him — I was just doing it for a laugh.

By now people had started to gather around Roy comforting him. He was saying through his pain, "Ben kicked me in … ", so people started looking at me screwing-up their faces and pulling angry ones. I quickly made off to my Mom's friend Maria's flat, still scared and frightened because I didn't know how much trouble I was in. I knocked on Maria's door shouting, "Maria, Maria!" She opened it and invited me inside.

I tell her that I have pushed Roy into the River Calder and that he had hurt his wrist badly, but that I was only doing it for a laugh. I didn't mean for him to be hurt! I genuinely didn't mean for him to be hurt. Maria informs me I have to go home and tell my Mom what has happened.

By now I'm even more frightened, at the thought of going and telling my Mom what I had done for a laugh and a joke. I sit and calm myself down before I leave for home, thinking how to make it sound not so bad — but I can't get away from the fact I did it, and it was my fault. I say goodbye to Maria then head out of the flat and start to make my way home from the West End area. As I was walking I saw Robbie and his uncle, who was of big build with a clean shaven head. I'd seen him when I'd been playing round there. He looked really angry this time, not like when I'd seen him before. His face was red and full of anger. I thought, "I'm going to be in for it now" and I was! He and Robbie approached me ...

"What the fuck have you done to Roy!?" he roared.

"Err, err, err ... I kicked him in the river for a laugh," I answered,

"Well, I don't think that's funny," he said.

I didn't know what to say or where to look, I felt one inch tall up against this man. I was terrified by his big frame and shaved head. He carried on for a minute but it felt like a lifetime, in fact it was one of the longest minutes ever.

The shouting finishes and he goes quiet and walks off, Robbie following close behind. I head off home down into Sowerby Bridge and under the railway bridge and over the River Calder and left on past the swimming baths and then over the road and up the steps. Then over the canal bridge and up Industrial Road, another one of the places I used to hang around sometimes, with a lad called Simon. He's okay, his parents have a nice house and it's bought, not privately rented or a council house.

Only a few hundred metres past the terraced houses on both sides and I'm in the grounds of Marton Heights. There are loads of maisonettes there, eight sets with six flats in each block. The first four blocks are on the right of the area with parking under the blocks and on the left is the little woods I play in, when you get to the end of the woods there's some stairs down to the next four blocks. My Mom's friend lives in the first block with her kids Carl and Zoë who are my friends, they're my age. My house is the third one along.

So only a minute or two and I'm going to be home for round two with my Mom. I don't want to go in, but I have to… I get to my block and through the outside door, down the stairs and into No.58, along the corridor past my sister's room and then after her's it's mine on the right.

I go straight to my room and start to feel frightened and scared again because my Mom is going to shout at me in a minute and I'm going to have to tell her about pushing Roy into the river with my feet for a laugh. I'm not sure she will think its funny, or a laugh!

I've been in my bedroom for no more than a minute and my Mom is shouting.

"Ben!"

"Coming!"

My heart is beating fast now but I get up to go in the front room and face the music and the shouting.

"Hello Mom," I say.

"Hi!" she replies.

"I got something to tell you but don't shout at me," I slip in as quickly as I can.

"What have you done?!"

"I kicked Roy in the river for a laugh but he hurt his wrist and I went up to Maria's because I was scared."

Mom didn't say much, to my surprise. I told her about Roy's uncle, the swearing and the shouting. Now she was annoyed with him and that made me feel at ease.

Tea was almost ready so I sat down and watched The Bill. The Bill was my favourite TV programme. By the time it had finished I was usually asleep.

Terry is my Mom's third husband, but he is cool, he takes me to football with him and spends time with us and takes us to the zoo or the seaside when he isn't working. Me and my sister like Terry. He carries me to bed when I fall asleep on the settee. I must have fallen asleep that night because I don't remember taking myself there.

2   Reading My Rights

I wake up early next morning and start to think about Roy and what I did to him. I've got to go to school and Roy is in my class, so is Robbie. I wonder if Roy will be in school because he was in a lot of pain but I'm not sure how bad it was, I know it looked bad to me.

I did the same thing every school morning: had breakfast, brushed my teeth, and waited for my sister so we could walk to school together. We would go out of the door of No.58, up the steps inside the maisonettes and out of another door into the fresh air. With the green grass bank in front of us, we would climb up it, across the car park and on to Hollins Lane, then down and round the winding bend, past the derelict buildings, over the River Calder, across the football pitch and up through the woods and on to Sowerby New Road. Then down to the lollipop lady and across the road into school.

Normally I love school, but not today. I know I've got to see Roy and Robbie and it will be the talk of the school. That scares me.

I go into the playground and everything seems normal, but as I get closer they are looking pretty serious, with the odd smirk.

I say, "Alright?"

Wayne is there and he says, "Alright."

Robbie says "Alright," too.

I ask about Roy. Robbie replies, "He broke his wrist. He has a blue pot on it now. He will be back in school tomorrow, a family member has rung the police..."

Oh no! Now I'm even more scared, now that the police have been called.

Roy wasn't in school so it must have been a terrible injury. The day passed without much more being said about the day before other than the odd gossip.

The final bell goes and I fly out of school and wait for my sister to walk home and to tell her about Roy's wrist. *The police have also been called.* She is so laid back and generally a good girl. I wait for a few minutes and she comes to the entrance. I can't wait to tell her. As we walk I explain about Roy and the police. She is shocked but tells me it'll all be okay, but I'm not so sure and I am scared to go tell my Mom in case of her shouting at me, so we walk back home slowly.

We get to the car park of Marton Heights and I can see my block. I slow down even more, in fear of the police being at my house. I scan the car park but no signs of any police cars so I head down the grassy bank and I get to our block and through the doors and down the steps and into No.58. Mom is waiting.

"Hello?" I call anxiously.

She summons me into the living room and tells me that a policeman has been to see her today and that we have to go to Sowerby Bridge Police Station for an interview!

An interview at the police station with a policeman, now I'm beyond scared and frightened. I feel like running away into the woods so no police will find me there, though I know I can't do that. She tells me to get changed and ready for the appointment at the police station about the GBH on Roy ... my schoolfriend is getting me done and it was only for a laugh! I didn't know how seriously he had hurt his wrist. Or that I had hurt him, it was just for a laugh but now this was serious.

So I got changed slowly and sat on my bed with my Liverpool FC covers on it and my Mickey Mouse hung on the wall.

My Mom shouts, "Right, come on Ben!"

I get up and take my time coming out of my bedroom knowing that we are heading for the police station but I eventually leave it for where my Mom is waiting for me in the hallway. Then we head for the door and through it up the steps and out of the block, and up the grassy bank to the car park where a Red Wharf taxi is waiting for us, with a smiling driver, to take us to the police station.

We get in and the friendly-faced driver asks us where we are going.

I interrupt my Mom and say, "The police station in Sowerby Bridge."

"No problem," he replies, and off we go.

As we drove there I was nervous, scared ... in fact, I was absolutely terrified. I'd never been to a police station before and I wasn't looking forward to it at all.

As we approached I noticed the police cars outside, it was a little building, not very big. We pulled up and my Mom paid the taxi driver his fare and we got up out of the car.

Now I'm so petrified, I don't want to go in because I don't know what to expect. We proceed through the front door and as we go in there is a desk with a policeman sat there. My Mom informs them we are here for an interview and tells them my name. He tells us to take a seat and that PC Naylor will be with us soon. Me and my Mom sit down and wait in suspense ready for his arrival. Now I was thinking, "I wonder if he's going to be cross with me" and "Am I in for *even worse?*"

We waited ten minutes. Then the door at the side of the desk opened and there *was* a policeman! I would say no more than 25-years-old with fair hair and about five feet two inches in height and of slim build.

He looked over towards me and my Mom and said, 'Hello, I take it you're Ben and this is your mother?'

I nodded and my Mom said, "Yes."

He escorted us to an interview room, me and my Mom sat at one side and PC Naylor at the other. He had two tapes, brand new with the plastic still on them, which he opened whilst looking at his paperwork. He then put them in the tape-recorder and asked if we were ready.

I nodded and my Mom said, "Yes".

PC Naylor pressed "Record" and the tape-recorder made a funny beeping noise. Then he began: "You do not have to say anything but it may harm your defence if you do not now mention something which you later rely on in court. Anything you do say may be given in evidence." He told me these were my "rights", I didn't know what he meant.

Next he started to ask me questions about what happened by the river. I told him I'd pushed Roy in and that I didn't mean to hurt him! He was my friend from school and it was a joke that had gone wrong. After he finished asking me questions he explained the dangers of the river. I said sorry and the interview was over pretty quickly. When he got the tapes out of the tape-recorder he sealed them up and signed them, then asked me to choose one. He then said he would be in touch about the GBH and to stay out of trouble in the meantime.

I said, "I will do".

"Yes, he will!" my Mom confirmed.

We left the police station and went home, had some food and I went to bed as I had school next morning. It had been a long, emotional day. My Mom didn't say much but better her not saying anything than shouting at me.

3   Fishing For Freedom

I woke up early the next morning and got my fishing rod and went over to Hill Top Dam and did an hour of fishing before school. I walked out of the door silently so as not to wake anyone. It was a fresh morning, I knew that as soon as I opened the main door of the maisonettes, with dew on the grass and the sky blue and sunny. I walk out of the front door and up the green grass bank, over the car park and left onto Hollins Lane and about 100 yards on the right is Hill Top Dam. As you turn up the path towards it you have to walk through some high grass, plus there is a lot of wildlife there including birds, frogs, ants, spiders and a lot of other things too.

I am walking up through the long grass and up the little embankment. I get to the side where you can look at the whole dam as it's not very big. As I walk I see a man fishing on the left, so I approach him and notice all his fishing stuff: loads of tackle, rods, poles and boxes inside boxes inside more boxes, tons of them. He had his bait in different tubs: maggots, luncheon meat, sweetcorn, bread. He had everything I could only dream of having.

I say, "Hello, I'm Ben..."

"I'm Dave nice to meet you, you're up early aren't you lad?"

I tell him I like to get up early, "Early bird catches the worm."

He smiles, looks at me and laughs which I find encouraging. I ask him about his fishing tackle and tell him, "I am an eager listener and learner when it has anything at all to do with fishing!"

Dave asked me what tackle I had? I told him a couple of hooks and a little tub of weights and one float. So not a lot to tell him about really. He sorted me a float and some weights, and a hook and told me to try it in a new way.

So I left Dave for my own spot and set up the float five feet from the hook and put a weight on either side of it and a smaller weight ten inches from the hook. Then I got what bits of tackle did have and put them all in one place, neatly so as not to lose things. I put a maggot on the hook and I was ready to cast. I cast my float out 20 feet from me and it made a soft impact as it hit the water. I watched it for a second as it submerged and then, like a jack-in-a-box, it popped back up out of the water.

Now it's a case of waiting and seeing what bites. I throw a few maggots around my float to bait the area, tips I have picked up off other fishermen with lots more tackle, equipment and knowledge. I sit there watching the float obsessively waiting for a bite for it to go under the water. It went under a few times but I wasn't quick enough to hook the fish. An hour went past and I had to get ready to go for school. I reeled my float in for the last time that morning and packed up.

Then I walked up to Dave and said, "You caught owt?"

He told me he'd caught half a dozen roach and perch. I was lost as to how he was catching all these fish when I was not catching anything!

I say, "Nice one Dave, I'll see you tomorrow if you're here?"

"Cheers, no problem and take care," he replies.

I walk off down the embankment and through the long grass to the road and turn left onto Hollins Lane, a hundred yards along then right into the car park and down the lush green banking. I go through the maisonette doors and down the steps into No. 58 silently, but my sister is up and so is my Mom.

I say, "Morning", with my little blue fishing rod in my hand.

They both say, "Morning", in reply, and I go off to my room to get ready for school.

It doesn't take me long and I'm ready to set off. As we get outside the maisonette it's sunny and the temperature is warm. We start to go up the banking and then I remember about Roy and what I had done to him and his wrist. He had not been in school yesterday but I'm sure he will be there today.

As we approach school by the lollipop lady I see Roy and his sister. I say to Natalie, "Look there's Roy and he has a big blue pot on." By this time we were ready to cross the road. The lollipop lady walks into the middle of the road and then waves us across safely, we walk across and Roy and his sister are just in front of us. I don't say anything to him, I just walk behind him into the playground where he disappears into the crowd and my sister does the same after saying "Bye". I just go to find Wayne and David and join in the football, soon forgetting about Roy.

The bell rings and we all go in sluggishly. As we get into class the other kids are gathered around Roy asking him questions about his wrist and why he has a blue pot on his arm, but this commotion soon passes as the teacher hushes everyone, orders us to our seats and hands out bottles of milk. We do some work and it's break in no time at all. We go straight to the playground and play football, but after a few minutes another teacher, Mr. Southwell, comes to us and says that the school are to play a football match against another school — The Sacred Heart School — and we are to look on the dining-room noticeboard at lunchtime to see if our names are written down on the team sheet which will be pinned-up there.

This makes us all excited as to who is going to make the team. The next period seems to take a lifetime but it is soon over. The bell goes and it's a race to the dining-room for me, Wayne, and David. We are told to slow down as we will hurt ourselves, so we do but as soon as Mrs. Hargreaves passes we speed back up again to full power. We hit the dining-room and go straight to the notice-board. I look at number one and it's me ... me! Now I'm over the moon, moving away from the board and into the dinner queue I can hardly contain my excitement. I'm the goalkeeper and *captain* of the team.

I sit down for dinner closely followed by Wayne who is in the team as well, he's in midfield and David who follows soon afterwards is in the team too. For the rest of the day we just talk about football and the team. This takes my mind of Roy's wrist and the day passes by without incident.

I finished school and waited for my sister. She arrives a minute after me and I waste no time in telling her about being in the team and that I was captain before we set off for the mile or so walk home. Before I know it we are there and I tell my Mom the same thing I had told Natalie nearly 50 times on the way.

The next morning comes and I'm up mega early, I'm going fishing and want to be there as early as I possibly can. I walk up to Hill Top Dam and look down over it.

Dave's already there in the same spot, fishing with all his tackle and equipment. I walk over and ask how he is. He tells me he's fine, and that he has brought me some tackle, thinner line, a few floats and some weights.

I say, "Thanks Dave!" and he puts the fishing line on my rod whilst promising me that I'll notice a difference. It's a lot thinner than my old line. I wait, excitedly but patiently. Dave finishes putting the line on in minutes, but I watch how he does it with a keen eye. As soon as he was done I was off to my spot to see if this would be a magic line. I set up my rod in double quick time as though it was a race to begin.

The first cast goes exactly where I want the float to be. I throw the maggots around it and within minutes I have my first bite. I strike and I don't believe it, I've hooked on the first cast. The fish doesn't put up much of a fight and it takes just seconds to get it in. It is a seven ounce roach, but I am happy to catch any fish. Over the next 45 minutes I catch another four, three roach and a perch. The change of line clearly helped me. I left it to the very last minute to leave because I was enjoying the new line and catching fish. I didn't want to go but I had to, so I rushed home to get ready.

A few weeks passed and I'd been fishing a couple of times a day most days before and after school. I'd almost become addicted to it. I loved it. I wasn't hanging round much with my friends, just fishing and I couldn't get enough of it.

I get home from school and my Mom is there to greet us and tell me that PC Naylor had been in touch. Roy's family are not going to be taking any further action against me. They have calmed down and realised it was just boys being boys, messing around, having a joke that went wrong.

It *was* funny apart from his wrist getting hurt and I am sorry about that. Now I am over the moon with happiness as I don't have to see P C Naylor or go to Sowerby Bridge Police Station again. I was so excited but Mom looked stressed, her and Terry had been fighting and arguing so maybe that's why? I went to my room and got changed quickly and gathered my bits of tackle and my little blue rod and headed straight out of the maisonette. I headed for the dam feeling on top of the world, now there were no more policemen to speak too.

As I walked up the embankment and looked over the dam it was peaceful, beautiful, and calm. The fish were topping the water catching flies, with shoals of roach all sticking together. There was no-one else at the dam so I went to my spot and set up my rod just how I had done for the last few weeks, apart from this time I didn't put a weight on ten inches from the hook, I put it nearer to the float so that when I cast my float out my maggot would drop through the water slowly and the fish would take it on the drop. I tried it with no weights and threw some maggots around the float. Boom, as it hit the water a fish was taking it. I caught one on the first cast, so that is how I continued to fish while the fish where topping. "Its brilliant," I thought to myself. I became obsessed with fishing and loved every minute I spent at the dam.

It's the six weeks holidays soon and my sister is going to High School when they are over. She only has a few days left in primary school and then she will be leaving and I'll have to walk to school on my own, but that doesn't bother me too much.

I have a game of football tomorrow against Sacred Heart School and I'm looking forward to it, as are all of the other boy's in the team. I am happy, very happy. I go fishing, I play football, I play in the woods, I have friends and I am the captain of the school football team.

4   Captain Ben!

The morning of our first football match I don't go fishing, instead I pack my boots in a bag and have breakfast to pass the time and wait for Natalie to set off with me to school. I am always ready first. But at least she is going to the High School soon, just two days left before we break up for the holidays.

I'm getting impatient now walking in the corridor outside our rooms shouting cockily, "C'mon I need to go and practice in the schoolyard, we have a game after school tonight if you didn't know!" Natalie opens the door of her room and we head straight out of the house. I start marching, with a spring in my step and am excited for what the day will bring.

We get to school in double-quick time I say, "Hello" to the lollipop lady and she replies, "Morning Ben." I tell her I'm playing for the school team and I'm the captain — I tell anybody who will listen. So she crosses us over safely like she has done every morning that I have been coming to school.

As soon as I'm at the other side of the road I take off running up the slope to the playground. Then slow too, a jog and then a walk as I get closer to the lads, to look cool of course. When I approach them, they are already talking about the game and how we will win! I join in the banter but before we know it it's time to go in as the bell is ringing. We haven't even kicked a ball this morning, we were so busy talking about what the score will be and who will get the goals. We are all excited and looking forward to the big game against our local school rivals. We go in sluggishly as always and sit at our classroom table.

Everyone is talking to each other, even me and Roy. He's forgiven me now so there is no atmosphere in the classroom anymore. Roy understands it was a joke and that I didn't mean to hurt him. So all is back to normal now that the weeks have passed and people have something else to talk about. The teacher comes in and asks everyone to take a seat and calm down, then we had our milk. Next we got on with our work, in and amongst talk of football and messing about.

Before we know it it's dinner time and the bell has gone. We get up and zoom for the classroom door and through it and outside as quickly as possible to play football: the sport we love and have been talking about all morning. I go in goal and the rest take shots at me and play One Man Champs. I am good in goal but not very tall, though I don't mind or even care. I can dive well and make saves no-one else could, or that no-one else would try on the gravel of the playground. I was always getting grazes and bruises from playing in goal.

Before we know it the bell goes and I slowly walk in for the afternoon lessons, but we know we're playing football after school and we have been waiting for what feels like forever for this day to come. Now we are only hours away from playing our first game. The afternoon drags on but we have work to do. We talk about football to pass the time quicker, plus we flick rubbers at each other using our rulers, and anything else to pass the time until the final bell goes. Now it has and that means only one thing: football!

We are the first out of the classroom and straight downstairs to the PE room where we are meeting to get changed before we walk up to Sacred Heart School, because we are playing on their pitch. We change into our blue kit then put on our shin pads and boots. Once everybody is ready we set off through the main doors of the school, turn right then up the snicket at the side of the school. We go up some steps and walk along to Quarry Hill, then right and across the road to

Sowerby New Road School football pitch, with it's lumps, bumps and slope towards the left hand goals. Above this is Sacred Heart's pitch, far better than ours, perfectly flat with no uneven parts.

The lads from Sacred Heart are warming up ready to take us on. The referee is from their school. We jog onto the pitch and start our own warm-ups and stretches, then passing the ball and various moves. Our teacher, Mr. Southwell, reminds us of everyone's position and tells us how we should play. I am not sure anyone listened, we just wanted to get on with it. How were we supposed to remember instructions when we were running around at a million miles an hour?

The games is about to kick off and we are ready. I shout, "C'mon lads!" and as I do the whistle goes. The game gets off to a good start, we score nice and early in the first half of 25 minutes each way, and the parents that came to watch us were cheering and chanting. Our team was jumping around with happiness. The other side got their heads down after the first goal went in but we were dominating them and the game from the off. We scored again after around 20 minutes to make it 2-0. When the half-time whistle followed I hadn't needed to make a single save.

The second half started and they played better forcing a few saves from me and then one went in! I was devastated but we were still in front and our heads didn't go down, the lads played their socks off and within five minutes we were 3-1 up! Again the parents were clapping and shouting and showing us their support for all the players in our team including me. Ten minutes left and we are winning when a few minutes later Wayne scores to make it 4-1. Wayne is a really good player as are all of the boys in our team. The whistle blows and it's full-time and we have won against our rival school.

After the game the teacher congratulated us all on having a great game, we were all as happy as Larry, and the parents came over and congratulated us too. There were about seven of them as well as the other boys' brothers and sisters who had come to support them.

No one came to watch me and tell me how proud they were. I will always remember that.

5 Winning

The six weeks holidays are here and my sister has left junior school and will be going to Sowerby Bridge High School when they are finished. This means I will be one of the oldest in our school and next year I will be going to high school too. As the holidays start I join Sowerby Robins Rugby Team, so I'm not bored in the holidays, plus I'm ten-years-old now and want to play rugby.

I've never done it before. I've only ever been to see Terry play for the Commercial Inn's rugby side. He plays there with his friends, Gary and Colin. He also plays football for Sowerby Bridge FC. He is only five feet eleven inches tall and of slim to medium build and hair slightly receding but he is as fast as lightning, he plays on the wing. His friends who play rugby also play in the football team with him as well as a man named Nev.

So on the Saturday I walk up to Burnley Road and onto the fields behind the Friendly Club. I liked training with the team and I liked rugby too, I was a good full-back as I was fast and small and not scared to make a tackle on anyone.

Fishing was the hobby I really loved though, and now we're into the holidays I can go fishing as much as I want and all day if I want to. This is heaven to me, going fishing at the dam, trying different methods and learning from other fishermen who go there including Dave. As I was there a lot of other people started fishing regularly and after talking between the older fishermen they decided to hold two competitions at the dam over the next few weeks. One was for the older fishermen and one was for the younger fishermen, and that included me. I was happy because I probably fished there more than anyone.

I was excited about my first competition but I soon forgot about it because I was playing in the woods, football in Marton Heights car park and on the little patch of grass next to it or doing something to keep me occupied with some of my friends who lived there.

One day in the holidays I went up to the dam and there were five men there, all people I recognised from fishing. There was another boy called Craig and he was with his dad. I got speaking to the people, Craig mainly, and he informed me they had some big empty black plastic rubbish bins on the back of one of the men's 4 x 4s with an open back on it and they were going down to the River Calder fishing. Whatever they caught they were going to keep and put it in the bins and release in Hill Top Dam so there would be more fish for us to catch there.

This excites me as I've never been to the river fishing before and I am keen to go with them and catch some different fish out of it. So I get Craig to ask his dad if I can go with them. He's not sure if I will be allowed to, but he will certainly ask if I can go with them. He goes off to his dad. I can see him pleading for me to go with them to the river, and I am praying his dad will say yes. His dad looks over at me and I turn away pretending I'm not looking and within seconds Craig is back. I was allowed to go and I was now more excited than ever.

We headed down the little embankment and through the long grass to the end of the road. Craig and I got into the back of the pickup truck, it was cool sat there.

Craig's dad jumps in then another man and the others get in their cars. We head off, the breeze in our faces and leave round the winding bend and down to the bottom, then pull up just on the right, the same way I walk to school. We get out of the back of the pickup and I get my fishing rod and stand to the side while the older fishermen get their stuff out of the car and off the back of the truck.

They all had seven foot fishing rods instead of the 12 foot ones they use on the dam. I asked Craig's dad why his rod was so small—he told me it was for spinning for trout. Well I don't have any spinners, I hardly have any tackle apart from what Dave gave to me. I told Craig's dad and he let me have some of his, telling me that if I lost it that's all I was getting. I say, "Thanks", and he smiles.

He goes in his pocket and pulls out a little green box, and in there are his spinners. I wait till the box is opened and see ones with spots on, ones with colours, some bigger than others. The bigger ones have three hooks, called a treble hook, and an oval metal spoon. I set my rod up and put my fishing line through the eyes on it. It didn't take me long as my rod is the cheap five foot blue one I've always had. It's for beginners or people who don't have much money like my Mom. The line was through the eyes and I had my only spinner in my hand. It had little red dots on it and was smaller than most of Craig's dad's other spinners. But I wasn't going to ask about using them now.

Everyone starts off towards the bridge I walk over to go to school five days a week. I've never been down here before without my sister and I have not told my Mom I'm coming here either, but I'm excited and can't wait to start fishing. Everybody splits up and goes and finds a bit of the river they like the look of. Two of the men take one black dustbin with them and me, Craig and his dad take the other one.

I start fishing about 30 metres down from the bridge heading towards Sowerby Bridge and Craig and his dad go a little further down the River Calder.

I cast my spinner across the river near to the other side, then I start reeling it back in immediately so it doesn't get snagged on the rocks or rubbish on the bottom, it's not the cleanest of rivers. I can't understand why people throw their rubbish in rivers when there are fish and other wildlife living there. I keep casting and retrieving the spinner for a good 30 minutes, casting up and down and across the river but I wasn't catching anything so I cast out for the last time and prayed and was willing the fish to take it. I reeled it in slowly and then faster but I didn't get a catch.

I got back on the path and headed in the direction Craig and his dad had with their dustbin. They were a few minutes walk down river nearer to Sowerby Bridge. When I got there I had a look inside the bin and saw a couple of fish in it.

"What are they?" I ask.

"Brown trout," says Craig's dad and I ask if I can get one out and have a look.

He says, "Yes" and I plunge my hands in and grab one of the fish carefully and pull it from the dustbin. It's about 12 inches long with small red spots all over it, it's a beautiful fish and bigger than the roach and perch I'd been catching at the dam. I put it back in the plastic dustbin and head off to find my own spot. I pass the other two men and ask if they have any fish in their dustbin and one man answers cheerfully, "Yeah got four, all brown trout."

I go closer and inspect the fish but without touching them, I just look closely into the dustbin. Their average size is between eight and 12 inches. This inspires me and I don't go far from where the two men we had come with were fishing, but not too close as fishermen can be touchy about people fishing close to them, or nicking their spot. I'm now on the cricket pitch but over the wall so as not to get seen as we were taking the fish out of the river and I get a feeling you're not supposed too.

Then I do the same as at the first spot. I cast over to the other side where there is a pub called the Puzzle Inn and start reeling back in but nothing happens. I am persistent and

keep going and it pays off after 20 minutes as a fish takes the
spinner about ten feet from the bank. It hits the spinner hard
and puts up a better fight than any other fish I had caught
out of the dam. I get the fish in to the side, pick it up and it's
a brown trout of about 14 inches.

I climbed back over the small wall and jogged up to the
two men with my fish, the first trout I ever caught and following the best fight. It was also the biggest I had caught so
far in my fishing days.

The men started smiling and said, "Well done." One of
them took it from me and got the pliers out because of the
three hooks. He gets them out in no time and hands the
fish to me to put in the dustbin with those they had already
caught. I don't know exactly how many because I wanted to
get back to the spot that I was fishing from, in case I caught
another and catching one trout had made me confident about
catching more.

I say, "Bye" then I start to run back to my spot, there's no
time to waste. I'm casting my spinner in the water and stalk-
ing the fish with my colourful spinner. It only seemed like
minutes and Craig came to tell me they were leaving. I cast
in one more time hoping for one last catch. It didn't happen,
but I was proud of the trout I had caught. We walked back
on towards his dad and one of the other men was there to
help lift the dustbin back up onto the pickup.

As we get there they are ready to go straight away. We don't
see one man, he must have already gone back or is still fishing. I don't ask. We get to the pickup and put our rods on
the back and then Craig's dad and another man put the big
plastic dustbin on the back with all the trout inside it.

We jump onto the back of the pickup, turning around and
head off back up the hill and round the bend and back onto
Hollins Lane. We pull up on the right at the bottom of the
grassy path to Hill Top Dam, jump out and wait for Craig's

dad and the other man to get the fish out of the back. Then they cross the road and carry the bin up the path and the little embankment. We get close to the water and wait for the fish to be released into their new home. I think there were eight or nine trout in our dustbin. As soon as they were released Craig's dad and the other man left me and Craig and went to collect his friend's dustbin. Craig and I waited patiently for them to return then rushed to see what was in it.

They had five fish, all trout, four of them, between seven and 12 inches. One is a lot bigger than the others, it's about 16 inches and weighs around two pounds. They release the fish and the adults talk, whilst I and Craig discuss the big fish his dad's friends have caught. Craig's dad calls Craig and tells him it's time to go. We say our goodbyes and walk back home and head for the bath as I stink of fish and have fish slime on my clothes from carrying them.

As I get into my home I see my Mom and she is upset, she and Terry have been fighting again and this upsets me because I like Terry, he's been better than my Mom's other boyfriends. She runs me a bath and asks where I have been all day? I tell her I have been fishing and how I have caught a trout, but she doesn't look interested in this topic, not many girls do either.

A couple of weeks have passed now and I have been fishing almost every day apart from rugby training and games. I am at home and I ask my Mom if I can go to the river on my own? She lets me and I am happy, but I don't have any spinners or bait. Instead I go to the kitchen sink and fill the bowl with hot water and add some washing-up liquid to make bubbles. Then I take it outside and pour it over the grass bank and wait for the worms to come to the top so I can use them as bait to try and catch something out of the river but I don't know what fish are in the River Calder.

I pour the soapy water over the soil several times until I get enough worms to last me a few hours as they fall off sometimes when you cast them into the water — as I have learnt from fishing at the dam. I also take some bread, these are things I've learned from other fishermen. I was going for the first time to the river on my own with my bread and worms and bits of fishing tackle. I had and my blue five foot fishing rod, it might have been cheap but I loved it.

I say goodbye to my Mom and make for the door, excited. I bust out of the block and into the sunshine and up the grassy bank and away to the river. I didn't catch any fish that day but I tried and I tried. I went home a bit disappointed but not too bothered as I enjoyed the peace and the surroundings by the river with the weirs and fast flowing water. It is only five or six minutes from my home. I loved Sowerby Bridge and the river and the dam and all the people there.

It's the day of the competition at Hill Top Dam. I am up early and raring to go, as my Mom has bought me some maggots and given me some bread as well. I don't eat breakfast, I just get ready and go, so I am early. There are a few older fishermen there and I walk up to them and say, "Morning". They say, "Morning" back to me and tell me I am early and that the kid's competition doesn't start till dinner time. I am not bothered by this, I watch the adult fishing competition looking for tips and fishing methods.

Dinner time comes and there are only three kids there, me, Craig and a boy I don't know. We started and I was fishing just how Dave had shown me. I ended up catching three roach and a perch and one of the trout we had put in earlier. That was enough for me to win the first ever kid's fishing competition at the dam. I was so proud of myself.

I got a trophy for winning the competition and a few bits of tackle that one of the men had bought to give to the winner. I couldn't wait to get home and tell my Mom and sister that I'd won the competition and show them what I had won. When I got there I went in and told my sister and she was happy for me. My Mom said, "Well done" and then after I had had a bath she took a picture of me with my trophy. A good end to the school holidays.

6 Moving to Mixenden

Back to school again and it's the first day. I'm walking there on my own. I didn't think I would miss my sister but I do. When I got there it was strange, being one of the oldest boys in school but I loved it, plus I got to see all the friends who I'd not seen in the six weeks holidays. There was lots to talk and the day was over quickly, then when school finished I had to go back home on my own.

For the first time I got a bit scared, going through the woods alone, in case anybody jumps out on me. There were not many people about and it felt lonely. As I got to the other side of the woods I was a lot calmer and I could see the bridge over the River Calder with the derelict buildings on the right, and then up and along the winding road back onto Hollins Lane, a right turn to the car park until I could see the grassy bank and the maisonettes.

My life was like this all through the next year. I'd walk to school, go fishing, play rugby, and mess about in the woods, play football in the car park and for my school. Me and some other friends who lived nearby would also be a bit naughty. We once knocked over a wall next to where people dried their washing.

My Mom had split up with Terry now so we was living on our own, me, Natalie, Mom and our dog Pippy. My older brother Robert had started coming to see us on weekends. He was 13, smoked, and lived my sister's dad and Molly, his wife. My real Dad has never had anything to do with me or my sister since my Mom left him when I was two-years-old. She once asked him for new shoes for us but he said, "No" because he was going on holiday and couldn't afford it. He used to beat up my Mom bad.

Robert started coming more and more and he tells us Molly hits him with a belt and she has been for ages. She makes him feel not wanted. I feel sorry for Robert, we go fishing sometimes when he comes over, he likes fishing too so that's good. But he's older than me and he's naughty sometimes and I am starting to follow suit.

I've left Sowerby New Road School and I'm going to High School after the holidays, I am nervous about this, but I will at least be able to travel to school with my sister again. But for now it's the six weeks holidays again and my Mom is moving us all to a new house back in Mixenden where I was born on June 15th 1983. I am eleven-years-old now. Moving house is the last thing I wanted, why would my Mom want to move us all to Clough Lane in Mixenden when it's so nice here?! I love the Hill Top Dam, I've been there more than I have at home over the last year. I'm gutted, really devastated, I don't want to move from Sowerby Bridge. I've got loads to do here and I am even catching trout from the river and going further and further up and down it looking for the best fishing spots. This is what I love, going fishing, football, rugby and playing in the woods with my sister and my friends.

All my friends are round here. The people from the dam! Craig! I can't believe we're moving, I feel sick. What about Wayne, he is my best friend. I am going to miss him and everyone else I know. I won't be able to see him or any of my other friends. Even now, everyone was going to different high schools apart from Wayne, and a girl called Kirsty who was my closest friend from Marton Heights.

The following day I told everyone I was moving house. They were as gutted as me, they said, "Stay in touch" and to "Take good care", and looked at me funny when I told them where we were moving to. I am not sure why I got that look but I was soon to find out…

It's the summer of 1994 and we have moved to Clough Lane in the middle of Mixenden. As soon as we got there I didn't like it at all. This wasn't Sowerby Bridge! I hate it, it's not like where I was before and there are little gangs of teenagers and loads of them too. I also have no dam to go to. I daren't even go out round here or I'll get bullied.

You can't just go out and feel safe walking around or playing like I did in Sowerby Bridge. I just want to go back to Marton Heights where I lived for years. I don't know anyone. I've had to stop playing rugby for Sowerby Robins, I'm not able to see the friendly faces I've known with everyone being on first name terms, even with the older adults that lived there. But most of all I miss Hill Top Dam and the River Calder and being able to sit there for hours fishing and watching fish top the water plus all the amazing wildlife that was there. All I long for is to move back to Marton Heights.

Natalie is always going to her friend's house. The friend lives at the top end of Mixenden so it's not bad for her because she she has friends here. They go to school together on the bus and I think they are even in the same class as each other at Sowerby High School. That is where I will be going after the holidays but I have to make it through them first. So I hardly see Natalie and plus she's a girl. Natalie has settled in quickly so she's okay and I am glad she is because I don't want her to feel the way I feel: trapped and compounded by the fact that I am too afraid to go outside.

My life was a nightmare now, I could not go out for fear of getting bullied or attacked because that sort of thing happened around Mixenden. It didn't in Sowerby Bridge, or I hadn't seen it. In Mixenden I feel isolated and alone: that I have no friends because they're all miles away. I miss them, and I miss Wayne, were always close before I moved away.

On one of the days my Mom comes into my room where I spend most of my time (or in the back garden away from the main road that's at the front of our house). She announces that Robert will be moving in with us. We are going to share a bedroom together. This excites me massively as I've been lonely having no friends around. Robert can play with me and this will make it better and I won't be as bored and I will have my brother with me, now our family feels more complete.

Robert gets dropped off with a couple of bin liners in his hands. That's his stuff, he must be moving in today. I run downstairs to meet him but he looks upset. My Mom says, "Hello" to him and we show him around our House of Horrors.

Maybe Robert will like it here, I don't know. I haven't seen much of him over the years and I don't' know where he lived? How he lived? What he does? Who he hangs around with? But I know he's my brother and I love him! No matter if we haven't seen each other that much, we are brothers we know that much and that is a special bond. Me and Robert go to our bedroom that we are going to share, it's cool to me because I've never had my brother living with me before that I can remember.

We unpack his stuff into draws and the area around his bed. I am curious to see what he has. I am happy he is back. He has "Fantasia" tapes and a small stereo with a couple of speakers so we can listen to them. I'd never heard of Fantasia before, so I ask to play it.

"Put it on!".

He does and we listen to the tapes for a few days and over this time we get to know each other better, and it started feeling like my older brother was here with me so I wasn't alone anymore. He told me stories of him living with my Dad and how Molly would hit him with a belt and he was treated different because she had three kids of her own. After listening to Robert I am just glad he is with us, especially if they are nasty to him. I don't know all the details, I just know he's with us now and sharing a room with me.

After a week I start going out with Robert around the Mixenden area and getting to know some of the other young people there. On one of the days a friend lent us his pellet gun and I went over to Mixenden Reservoir with it. There were people in canoes, something to do with a youth club. I shot at a couple them. I am not sure if I hit the canoes but they all turned round and started shouting at me to stop it and saying that I was going to be in trouble. I ran home and hid the gun. Then I just went into our bedroom and listened to some of Robert's tapes as he was out with people he knew.

I did not think much of the pellet gun incident until a policeman came and knocked on the back door of our house and asked my Mom if I had one. He recognised me and gave me a telling-off and said it was dangerous, but after that he was more concerned with flirting with my Mom. I quickly went up to my bedroom waiting for her to come and shout at me, but she didn't.

After a while me and Robert were starting to argue and getting physical. After a while of sharing rooms with him it drove me to think, "Fuck it, I'm going out, I'm not going to stay in as much as I have been doing anymore, I'm so bored with this house and area its driving me crazy." So I suggested to Robert we go to Sowerby Bridge fishing! We asked my Mom if it was okay for him to take me there on the bus. She agreed and we get my fishing tackle and headed-off for the bus to Halifax. When we got there we then looked for the bus stop for Sowerby Bridge, for the bus back to heaven.

The bus arrives, my brother pays our fares and we go upstairs and sit near the back because that's what cool kids do, right? We soon arrive and get off across from Kwiksave then walk down to the River Calder and set up my blue fishing rod. I'm fishing for brown trout and the odd grayling, until our worms run out that is.

I didn't want to go home to my Mom's, I wanted to stay here forever and never return to Mixenden. So instead of going home we decided we would walk round Sowerby Bridge and along the canals. I liked the canal by the mooring where all the beautiful barges are with all their pretty colours and individual designs. All of them are different with their own names, pretty flowers on them, and bicycles tied down on top of some of them as well. Then we got to some derelict factories at the side of the River Calder where there's also old tunnel type bridges across the river. The factories had holes through their rotted wooden floorboards. It was dangerous but we still went inside and messed with the cast-off tables and chairs. Then we made fires in there. We was unsupervised and doing what most kids would do when left alone for long periods of time. As it got later we knew it was time to go as it was getting dark.

We made our way home the same way that we came. Our Mom asked where we had been, and why did we smell of smoke. We just said we had a fire by the river, so she asked us where we got a lighter from? We told her Robert had bought some matches. She wasn't impressed at all, she knew we had been up to something but couldn't prove it and I am not sure she was all that bothered.

We had our food and went up for a bath to get rid of the smell of smoke and the dirt on our hands and faces. Robert listened to his music while he waited for his turn in the bath. So this is what we did all summer, going to Sowerby Bridge as much as possible. But instead of going fishing we would just take the rod and tackle and hide it when we got there. Then we would look for stuff to do like going into old factories and breaking things, having fires, it was dangerous a lot of the time but we didn't care, we wasn't in Mixenden and that's all that mattered.

As the weeks passed we were becoming naughtier and I was having the odd cigarette here and there with my brother. My Mom recently told us Robert will be going to Sowerby High School. So that meant I was safe going to school as both my sister and brother would be on the same school bus as me.

School term starts and I'm in Mr. Trent's form 7.3. Wayne is in 7.1 with Mr. Pearson the PE teacher. I go to school every day and I like it, though not as much as I used to love Sowerby New Road Junior School. But I soon make friends with a boy called Matthew, I used to sit near him and hang around with him sometimes, he used to live on Manor Drive. I've been to his house after school sometimes because Robert has friends he goes around with now, so I don't get to see so much of him other than when I'm on the bus to school. We get different buses home because I go to my friends or hang around Sowerby Bridge market after school.

I've started playing rugby again at school and I love it and the physical contact because it's a way of releasing the anger that was building up inside me. I feel older after all the things we did in the summer.

I've also started playing in the football team again, but I'm a striker now not a goalkeeper, as I didn't grow much taller and got lobbed three times in my last game for Sowerby New Road against Christchurch. We lost about 8-0. Wayne is in the football team as well, in midfield. But in class I am being cheeky to the teachers and messing around being a general pain in the arse. So the teachers have decided to move me to Mr. Pearson's class on account of my behaviour getting worse. Well I loved this, I knew Wayne was in that form and couldn't wait.

Moving to Mr Pearson's class came and I couldn't wait to get back with Wayne. He's hilarious, funny, a joker and a prankster. But soon I was to realise why the teachers had moved me. It was so Mr Pearson could threaten that if I didn't behave well I wouldn't be picked for the football team or rugby team! It was a good idea for a couple of months but I soon got fed up and easily bored with the lessons apart from PE. I was also being naughty at home and Robert and Natalie and I were starting to have physical fights by now. Mainly me and Robert, but Natalie would always stick up for him and he would do the same for her.

Mom would get upset because of our behaviour, our fights, and not listening to her. She was going out more and more leaving us for days or nights when she was out drinking with her friends or doing part-time jobs. Me and Natalie tried cannabis in a bucket bong once when Mom was out, this made us violently sick, throw a whitey as people say. We shared a toilet being sick into it at the same time; it wasn't a pretty sight that's for sure. I hated it and so did my sister. I thought I won't be doing this again in a hurry.

I was being naughty at school and naughty at home. My days at the dam seemed a long time ago now, I seemed to have gone through a lot over the time that Robert had lived with us and I'd been getting naughtier and naughtier since moving to Mixenden. I did not like it at all, I couldn't get used to Mixenden and my world had been tipped upside down.

7 Abandoned

As it came to Christmas 1995 my Mom had had enough and couldn't take it anymore. She left one day in the beginning of December, the 2nd to be precise. She didn't say that she wasn't coming back.

It got late and me, Natalie and Robert were watching TV and asking each other, "Where do you think she is?"

Maybe she was at Paula's, the house of one of her friend's who lived at Marton Heights with her two kids Carl and Zoë.

"What time will she be back?" I ask my siblings.

"We don't know!"

"Did she say she was going somewhere?"

"No!"

I was getting hungry by this time and I didn't know how to cook, so I looked through the kitchen cupboards and there was plenty of food but all frozen or something we didn't know how to make.

There is always food in our cupboards and the house is always spotless. I leave the cupboards and just get the biscuit tin out, there are custard creams and bourbon chocolate ones in it, lots of them, my Mom must have recently filled it. I eat them all and still my Mom isn't back from wherever she is.

It was really late now and I was tired and becoming worried so I went to bed leaving my brother and sister downstairs. I lay in bed wondering where my Mom was, and if she was okay and well. I must have drifted off to sleep.

After I woke up in the morning I went downstairs and my Mom still wasn't back. By now we are all worried and fretting, my stomach is rumbling because I'm hungry, I only had biscuits for tea. As I go to the room Robert and Natalie are still there, I'm not sure if they went to sleep or not.

I ask, "Is there is any news, has my Mom rung?"

"No" is the answer to each of my other questions about whether there is any news.

I'm scared, we all are. We just hang around the house waiting for our Mom to return, but she didn't and we were hungry. We just ate biscuits and had cheese sandwiches and jam sandwiches too. Tea time came and still no return! We were getting terrified and all sorts of different thoughts were starting to cross our minds now, we were getting more upset as time went on. I think it's then we realised she wasn't coming back.

We didn't know what to do, we just watched TV and messed about in the back garden until it was dark and cold. Then the night came and we decided between ourselves if she doesn't come home by tomorrow we will ring the police using 999. The next morning arrives and I dart downstairs to see if my Mom has returned … she hasn't. Robert, Natalie and myself all agree we should now call 999 and tell the police. We will say our Mom hasn't come home and hasn't been back for days now and we are really worried.

I had to be brave and ring 999. I told the operator man, "My Mom hasn't been home for two days and we are worried about her!" The man asks me how old I am, I tell him I'm 12-years-old, that my brother is 14 and my sister 13. He tells me he will be ringing back shortly and to stay by the phone. I say, "Okay" and put it down.

I tell Robert and Natalie what he has said to me and that he will be ringing back shortly and we have to wait by the phone. It doesn't take long for a social worker to call us back.

I answer the phone and say, "Hello'.

The social worker says, "Hello" as well and then starts asking me questions.

"How old are all of you children?"

"What has happened?"

"Where is your Mom?"

"How long have you been alone?"

I answer as best I can and he informs me he will be at our house soon. He says, "Goodbye" and I put the phone down.

I am scared, we all are really. What is he going to do when he gets here? Is he going to be baby-sitting us till my Mom returns from wherever she has gone? We are all nervous about what is going to happen. We are waiting for half-an-hour for him to come. Then a car pulls up outside the gate of our house. A man gets out of it and looks at the numbers on the doors and makes for ours: this must be him.

8   Move #1

We can see the social worker through our net curtains in the front room. He knocks on the door and we all go to it not knowing what he's going to say or what he's going to do. We open the door and he asks if I'm Ben? Then he asks Robert and Natalie in the same way, and they say "Yes" to his question. We let him in and go to the front room where we all sit down on the settees.

He starts again with the questions.

"When was the last time you saw your Mom?"

"Does she normally do this?"

We answer him but he can see we're all scared and he tries to reassure us everything will be fine and that we will be looked after. He makes some phone calls in the garden and speaks for a little while to different people then he comes back inside the house and into the front room. He asks, if we have any relatives we could go and stay with? I say, "No!" and Robert says, "No!", but Natalie says her friend will let her stop at her house.

I'm not sure which friend's house she went to but she got took there by another social worker and me and Robert were left with the man who originally came. He made phone call after phone call trying to find us accommodation in a children's home or a foster placement. After what seemed like hours, he said, "Right, I've found you a children's home in Ovenden called 'Cousin Lane'."

Robert and I looked at each other with fear in our eyes not knowing what to expect when we got there.

"Will we get bullied?"

"Will they like us?"
"Are they friendly?"
"Will they accept us?"

We get a few belongings together and say goodbye to Pippy the dog who I will miss very much. I loved Pippy, she was the nicest dog I've ever met with her temperament, she was a beautiful Border Collie crossed with an Alsatian, with long black furry hair. We head for the social worker's car and Robert jumps in the front seat and I jump in the back.

We drive to Cousin Lane, it only takes five minutes because it is just two miles from our house. We pull up outside the home, halfway along the lane. It's a big house, two knocked into one, with red bricks and grass around it with a path. It also has green privets surrounding it that have been trimmed really nicely.

As we enter a member of staff comes to greet us and shows us to the staff office. In there is one other member of staff. They ask us more questions and then show us too our separate bedrooms. We each have our own, I have the one on the end of the corridor facing the back garden, the room is quite small with a window to the left and a single bed under the it. Robert's room is half-way up the landing. Once we had put our things that we had with us in our rooms we went and met the other residents. There were about five other young people there and they were all friendly to me and Robert, but this wasn't my home.

All the other kids smoke here too like Robert—and me sometimes. So after the staff had left us in the main room, we got talking with the other young people there and became friends quickly. Before an hour was up it seemed like we had known each other a long time. They showed me and Robert where they smoked and told us things they would do when they got bored or felt mischievous. They told us that if they didn't want to go to bed then they would refuse to go to their rooms and let the staff chase them around, because the staff can't hit them! It was all a new world to me, all I'd known until then was fishing, rugby, football, the dam and the woods.

But it was fishing I was missing the most, something I hadn't done for a long time. I missed going to the dam and the river and seeing my friends.

So the night comes and it's time to go to sleep. Everyone has a set bedtime and the time depends on your age. A member of staff calls me and tells me to go brush my teeth and to get undressed and into bed. I say, "'Night" to Robert and then everyone else and make my way up to my room. I get inside and close the door and sit on my bed in a daydream asking myself if this is real? Is this really happening to me? Last night I was in my own bed with my own covers in my own surroundings and now I'm in a children's home feeling all alone and wondering, "Whatever's going to happen to me?"

I start to cry and lie on my pillow face down as I do so. So no-one can hear me crying like a baby. I just wished I was in Sowerby Bridge but my wish didn't come true, just the start of the nightmares to come.

I cried myself to sleep that night in Cousin Lane.

9 The First Cut is the Deepest

I woke up early that next morning thinking I was still at home. But I wasn't, so I dragged myself out of bed and went downstairs to find Robert but he wasn't up.

One of the staff asks if I'm okay and if I slept well?

I say, "I'm okay", I'm not really — but I don't want to tell anyone how I feel and that I cried myself to sleep last night. Instead I put a brave face on and tell the staff everything is okay.

They ask if I want to go to school today.

"School?" I say.

"Yes!" says the member of staff. We will drop you off and pick you up after school."

I say, "Yes" and they tell me to have breakfast and get changed into my uniform.

I go up and get changed and ready myself for school. I don't eat breakfast, I just want to get out of Cousin Lane and to be in familiar surroundings.

I get to school and the member of staff tells me to wait at the main gate after school and says that is where I will be picked up from and I then go into school. But I go straight out of the other side and down to the smoker's corner at the bottom of the football pitch by the phone box. I bought a single cigarette off another pupil with some of the money Cousin Lane had given me for school.

The day passes and I've been told-off several times because I wasn't paying attention, or I was messing about or not concentrating. The teachers don't know what I'm going through: that I'm now living in a children's home because my Mom left us home alone for two days just eating biscuits, cheese sandwiches and jam ones as well. Or that I cried myself to sleep last night and that it was my fist night in the care of social services, also I still don't know if my Mom is dead or alive, so forgive me for not concentrating!

I sit wondering if they know any of this, that I'm just a broken-hearted little boy whose world is caving in around him and that I am just starting at a new stage in my life? It's not the life I had in Sowerby Bridge, it's totally different and that was only my first night.

School was over for today and I went and waited where the staff had told me to for my lift back to Cousin Lane. I thought about running-off but my heart sank as I realised I had nowhere to go. I thought about going and making a den at Hill Top Dam — the place where all my fondest memories and the happiest days of my life were. Then I considered the old factory down by the River Calder, but I was too scared to go there on my own and I had no food, money, or lighter to make a fire to keep myself warm.

As I'm stood in a daydream surrounded by my own thoughts, a horn beeps right outside the main entrance and makes me jump! I'm edgy enough as it is. It is the same member of staff to pick me up, so I get in the car and he says, "Have you had a good day?".

I thought, *"Are you having a laugh?"* quickly followed by, *"No, I've had the worst day. I've not been able to concentrate with all the things going on in my head and life. Plus moving to another place where I don't know people. Living with five other young people and two to three strange staff I don't know and have never seen before."*

But I replied, "Yes, not that bad" still with a brave face.

We get back to Cousin Lane and I go straight to find Robert but he wasn't in, he was out with his friend who lived near Cousin Lane with my Dad and Molly and her three kids. So

I got changed and went back downstairs to see if anyone else was about for me to mess with. There was one boy called James. I don't know why he was there and I didn't ask. He was a nice boy, friendly and of a similar age to me, 12-years-old. We played Connect Four for what seemed like hours and it kept me occupied.

Robert came in later with another boy from the children's home, he said, "Hello" as he did so but it seemed like he didn't really care. It seems that he was okay, not like me. I was feeling entirely lost and alone — the same feeling I had when I first moved to Mixenden. I went up to my room and started crying again, thinking "*I can't take this not being at home,* and staying here makes me feel so alone my brother's just getting on with it or at least it seems that way to me."

I smash a light bulb that's in my light socket and start cutting myself with the broken pieces of glass, not too deep just enough to take my mind off everything else that is going on. It seems to release something, but I'm still crying. It was the first time I self-harmed. One of the staff comes into my room and is taken aback by what she sees from a 12-year-old boy. She tries to take the bulb off me but I don't let her have it and she knows — if she tries getting it by force — someone's going to get hurt and I don't care if it was me, I am past caring. So she shouts for another member of staff, Larry to come and join her in getting the bulb off me. He came running up the stairs and into my room to support the other member of staff. I just said I would give up the bulb myself because I was calming down a little. Then I threw it out of the window.

The woman cleaned the cuts on my legs and dressed them for me while Larry picked up all the bits of broken bulb. They have a chat with me and reassure me that everything will be fine, it just takes time to sort things out. Then I ask them to leave me alone and say that I'm going to go to sleep as I'm exhausted.

After the last 72 hours it feels like I've been on a terrifying rollercoaster which I cannot get off. They left my bedroom and I shut the door and started crying again. We'd still not heard anything from my Mom, I'll ask about her when I get up in the morning but I'm sure someone would have told me if she had returned home or if anything had happened to her. I cry myself to sleep again that night as well, face down in to the pillow to drown out my sobs.

10 Heartbreak

The next morning comes and I'm up early, but not in a good way like at Marton Heights. I got up early when I was at Cousin Lane because I couldn't sleep properly, my mind just seemed to consume me and no matter how hard I tried I just could not switch off. I got up early at Marton Heights because I couldn't wait for the day to start and I could go fishing and was happy, and loved the dam and the wildlife. Here, I hadn't been eating well either.

I go downstairs and a member of staff calls me into the office and tells me my Mom is safe and well and has returned to the family home. He tells me she has been in Blackpool at a friend's house. I ask enthusiastically if Robert and I are going home—for the first time in days I feel excited about something.

"No," he says.

"Why?" I ask him.

"She's not willing to have you both back just yet."

My world comes crashing back down again, and this was to be a turning point in my life.

My heart breaks—smashed into a million tiny pieces around my feet. I may have been naughty at home, but I'm not sure I should be staying here. I go into self-destruct mode and hit things, break things and call my Mom all the names under the sun because I am angry and ready to explode. I become volatile, upset, heartbroken, confused all at the same time.

"My Mom doesn't want me."

Well what the fuck! They ask me if I am going to school today? I tell them "Fuck off you pricks, I hate you!" Then

I storm out and go walking up to the fields at the back of Cousin Lane and across some land that looks over Mixenden.

"I hate Mixenden!"

11 Kicking-Off

I sat there all day trying to think, but I was numb, I didn't know what to suppose or feel anymore. I was getting cold and I must have been sitting in the same spot for hours because it was almost dark and I left the children's home that morning.

I get up and head back there, my new "*home*"

"I'm a mess," I thought, "*I can't go back there, but I have nowhere else to go either.*" I get back to Cousin Lane and go to my room. One of the other young people is "kicking-off". He is shouting, swearing, and breaking things. I go out of my room and see what's happening and now there are two residents kicking-off! So I think "*Fuck it,*" and join in as well, so now there are three of us doing the same thing.

As any kid who's grown up in care will know, kicking-off is an all-encompassing and somewhat melodramatic term used by adults who are paid to "care", describing any disruptive behaviour by a child or young person. The chances are, by kicking-off, they are actually simply trying to tell you something. Often this behaviour will include shouting, swearing, throwing stuff and basically any behaviour which the young person uses to hide their fears and feelings. It, can be feared by adults, provoked by adults and definitely avoided by adults — if they are willing to explore why the young person is demonstrating this "behaviour", through talking to them and listening to what they have to say.

Needless to say, the staff are not amused by this episode and are quick to tell us they will be ringing the police if we carry on. I calm down quickly at the mention of the police. I don't want to be locked up as the staff member keeps threatening us, telling us this will happen if we carry on and don't go to bed. So with that I retire and go to my room as its late now and past my bedtime.

I messed about most days after that and was disruptive almost all of the time. Now I was angry, feeling out-of-control and starting to rebel. I didn't want to listen to the staff—they were not my parents. I only have a Mom and she couldn't handle us all being just a single parent, it was very difficult for her and I understand that.

It gets to the 10th of December and I am feeling volatile. My little head is a mess with emotions and it's been a heart-breaking couple of weeks, and I've had enough. So me and two other residents decide we are going to kick off tonight and will be refusing to go to bed, no matter what! Regardless of what the staff say, no threats will be working tonight!

I'm one angry young man ready to hit out at everyone and everything. I don't know whether I'm coming or going. Tea time arrives and we are already messing about running in and out of bedrooms—the staff hated that! As the night went on we were throwing stuff around in the main room of the children's home.

The staff knew they were going to be in for a long night. It comes to my bedtime and I am not going to bed!

The staff say, "Bed now, Ben!"

I say, "Get fucked! I'm not going to bed tonight!"

Then another resident says he isn't going to bed either. We go upstairs and hide in another resident's room, now there are three of us in one bedroom and none of us are going to bed or to sleep tonight. I've had enough of being told what to do by people I don't know. None of the staff talk to me and ask me how I'm feeling and about my problems. They just treat us all the same, I needed love and affection and I can't remember the last time anyone told me they loved me.

The member of staff comes to the door and demands that we open it and go to our rooms. We tell her to "Fuck off!"—we aren't going to bed. Then we bombard her with abusive and inappropriate language. She goes away from the door to get another member of staff, so we dart back down the stairs and into the main living-room. The staff member comes in and tells us we need to go to bed or the police will be called and we'll all be spending the night in a cell. This didn't put us off this time, it worked the first time—but not this time. We became more abusive to them and eventually the staff member snapped and said, "That's it, you can spend the night in the cells."

We tell them, "Go and do it!" and with that the staff member turned and left the room and went to the office and rang the police.

So we carried on with our bad language, bombarding the male member of staff that was left in the room with us. Then he'd had enough, you could see the anger in his face building, he was becoming angrier and angrier with every word we shouted.

He turned and left the room as it was showing.

12 Arrested

Within five minutes the police were at the door, and they were soon informed of what we had been doing, being told that we are refusing to go to bed and being abusive to the staff.

The little policeman with glasses grabs me and puts his handcuffs on me to my rear and leads me out to his waiting Astra patrol car to put me inside. The other boys had been arrested too and are being led to another waiting patrol car to take them to the police station.

This was my first time being arrested. I was terrified of what was to come as I'd never been to Halifax Police Station before. I wasn't sure what was going to happen to me. As we got near to the place the police officer with the spectacles on that looks like the Milky Bar Kid's dad tells me, "It's, 'Yes Sir, No Sir', when you get to the custody area you little bastard."

This scared me greatly and put real fear into me. Now I was going to do exactly as he said! I didn't want to provoke him anymore and make him any angrier than he already seemed.

We pull up outside the back of Halifax Police Station where he tells me, "Get out of the car!", then pushes me about a bit and gives me a couple of slaps for good measure! Then, repeating exactly what he said minutes earlier in the car, he tells me again, "It's, 'Yes Sir, No Sir', when you get to the custody area you little bastard."

The officer then presses a button on the wall in the foyer. The button beeps then the door opens making a clicking sound, and then the officer pushes it open and leads me inside were there is another door to go through with metal bars. Once we're inside we wait for that door to open, then in front of us is the desk were the sergeant sits and books people into custody.

He tells the officer to put me in a holding cell. They tell me I'll wait there until he's booked in the person already stood at the desk. I am scared and the roughing-up hasn't helped me, it's only made things worse and I now feel I don't like the police very much and certainly won't be trusting them if this is how they treat young people.

I'm just a young boy who has lost his Mom: I need *help*— not locking up. Now here I am, my first time in police custody, being bullied by a full grown man who has no time for me other than to rough me up. Is he teaching me a lesson so I don't come back? I'm now in the holding cell weeping, I sit stiff and still feeling so scared I daren't move. I feel that if I do move I may get roughed-up more by this little specky bully who loves the power of his uniform!

After a few minutes the sergeant asks PC Lemonhay to bring me to the desk, and once we are stood in front of it he asks him why I've been arrested. PC Lemonhay then explains to Sergeant Whiting the reasons for my arrest, although he manages to forget to tell him about the slaps he has given me. Sergeant Whiting says he authorises my detention, and asks me if I understand why I have been arrested?

I say, "Yes, *Sir*!"

He then asks me for my name,

"Ben Larkin, *Sir*" I reply.

He then asks me for my date of birth.

I tell him "15/06/1983, *Sir*."

He then follows up that question by asking me my address.

"Cousin Lane Kids Home, *Sir*!"

After that he tells me I will have to wait for an appropriate adult to come so he can give me my rights! Then he tells PC Lemonhay to take me to cell No.9.

You turn right at the desk then walk down the corridor and follow it to the left-hand side and its half-way up the corridor on the left. A blue door with a little circle of glass also known as a "peep-hole" with a hatch just below it.

"In you go," says PC Lemonhay!

I walk into the cell, it is dark and creepy. No lighting is on. The door slams! I am left alone and scared in this cold dark cell, for the first time ever in my life. I look around. There is no mattress or blanket and there are big square blocks of thick reinforced glass to let the light in, but there no light because it was dark outside. The cell is freezing and I don't like it.

I start to cry and think about crazy things like strangling myself with my pants, head-butting the wall, the door, punching walls, but I am scared to move and dare not make a noise. A few hours pass and the hatch opens and the detention officer says, "Emergency Duty Team, part of social services, we're here for your rights to be read. Your Mom has refused to come to the police station and be your appropriate adult and Cousin Lane don't want you back there either."

He opens the door of the cell and leads me back to the custody area where the man from the EDT is waiting for me. I walk up to where he was standing and say, "Hello!"

"Hi, Ben." he replies. "Are you okay?"

I think he must be able to see I'm just a frightened little boy.

They read my rights to me and ask me to sign the bail sheet. Then they tell me I'm going to be charged with an offence under section 4 of the Public Order Act, and I am to be bailed to the care of the local authority. As we make our way out the duty social worker tells me it only took so long for me to be released out of police custody because they had no place for me to stay. That was until they found some emergency foster parents in Walsden near Todmorden about eleven miles from Cousin Lane.

13   And So, the Moves Begin …

We made our way to Walsden in the social worker's car, it took about 35 minutes. On the way I'm nervous as I don't know what to expect, I am not sure if they are going to be nice to me as I'm not their son. They might have kids of their own, how will I fit in with this family that doesn't know me. I am apprehensive about going to a new place with people I don't know and who have never met before.

This is a lot for me to take in. I'm still only 12-years-old and this is my fourth move, my second to a strange place. But this was just the start of my moving around different homes.

The next one was to a family member's house in Brighouse for a couple of weeks. She tried her best with me but I just didn't like being away from Halifax and Sowerby Bridge. She didn't get hardly any help or support from social services while I was with her, it felt like they just dropped me off on her and expected my aunt to sort everything out. It was a lot to ask of her. Plus all my friends were in and around Halifax. I only lasted a couple of weeks as I kept going missing for days at a time, then I'd usually be brought back by the police. It was in these times I found myself sleeping rough for the first of many times. I would often find myself sleeping in Halifax Bus Station toilets in a cubicle. I would lift my feet up so it would look like nobody was in there. Other times it would be in the paper recycling bins in Netto's car park, it felt safe inside the bins and was more comfy than the bus station.

Is it right that no one is looking for me or letting me sleep in recycling bins or the bus station toilets? I cannot remember one member of staff ever looking for me or finding me. These were some of my most frightening nights sleeping on my own and feeling that no one loved me. It was a lonely existence being on my own but it seemed better than where I was staying, I was confused and felt no support from anyone other than my auntie. I wished people would look for me and show me some attention and support to help me through the bad times but it never happened.

I used to be terrified sleeping on my own in strange places. I knew I was at risk from older people who could abuse me. I used to think about that and what they might do to me as I was only a kid and in real danger. But I was streetwise and I hoped that would see me through the bad times ahead.

So it wasn't long until I was moved on to another family member's house. I was still causing mischief but I managed to avoid any trouble with the police for a couple of months. But I would still find myself sleeping rough and going missing for days at a time. I would often sneak into other children's homes and stay there. My family members tried to keep me occupied but that was only going to last for so long as I had hardly any support or help with why I was behaving like I was and what would make it better, no one asked.

On the 25 February 1996 I went to Mixenden to go to my Mom's house to see her as I'd not done so in a couple of months and I wanted to know where Robert was. I'd been moved from Cousin Lane to foster parents and then to my family member's in Brighouse then to another family member's, plus I had been sleeping rough and I'd lost track of where Robert was. I got to my Mom's but she wasn't in, so I was walking to the bus stop.

While I was on my way I saw some older youths who were friends with my brother and a few other people I'd met when I used to hang around with him. I started talking with them, they were older than me but that wasn't a problem. So I stayed with them and they were talking about nicking a car. I've never been in a stolen car (TWOC sometimes called twocking[2]) but I was certainly up for it as I didn't want to go back to my family member's place.

All those fears of walking in Mixenden had gone and I felt part of the crowd and Mixenden didn't seem such a bad place now. The older boys twocked the car and picked me and another boy up. We went joy-riding in the stolen Cavalier SR 130, apparently the best car to TWOC as they are easy to take and fast.

We go joy-riding up on The Withins — a place just above Mixenden on vast moorland, popular with all young car thieves. We travelled all around the areas near Mixenden until, eventually, it was late and no other cars were on the road apart from taxis and police cars.

Well what do you know we are going back up towards The Withins when suddenly a police car is right up behind us.

"Oh shit!" the driver shouted.

He starts speeding up, but we are unable to go too fast as there is still some snow on the roads. There was a short chase and the car was rammed into a wall by the Volvo T5, and they then boxed us in against it. By this time there were four or five police cars (Astras and Volvos). The police officers pulled us from the car forcefully and handcuffed us. With me being so small the officer who first pulled me out handed me straight over to a woman police officer. I was glad he did because she put me straight into the back of a Volvo.

As I sat there looking out of the window I saw police officers give a few punches to the older boys and start being rough with them. This time I wasn't sacred like the last time I got arrested. Now don't get me wrong, I wasn't looking forward to it. I had been here a few months ago and it was an ordeal for me — but I didn't feel scared I actually liked being

---

2. Twocking is shorthand for 'taking [a car] without consent'.

part of this group of older boys. I thought, "If they're going to get locked up all the time then that's what I will do!"

So, on that day I got charged with aggravated TWOC and a week or so later I was still at a family member's house in between being missing the odd night. On this particular day I travelled to Halifax from Brighouse and met up with my brother in the bus station and he was with a couple of people from the car incident and another group I didn't know. We stayed around the bus station smoking and drinking. Then we walked around Halifax town centre, drinking more and more and getting louder and louder. It doesn't take long before we are drunk on White Lightning.

We used to get three litres of White Lightning and take it in turns seeing who could down most in one go. Whoever could drink most got most. So I am really drunk at this point as this is my first time getting pissed. I was way drunk, more than the older boys, I was falling about and I had slurred speech and wobbly legs, finding it quite difficult to walk.

Along with seven other young people I get on the bus to Mixenden. We were loud and some of the people with us were being aggressive and shouting. Half-way there the bus driver stops the bus and manhandles one of the boys off of it, the other lads react and start to hit the driver. Then some of the passengers get involved and it begins to escalate and I and the other boys start throwing bricks off a wall through the bus windows, breaking them and in the process showering other passengers with shards of glass.

It doesn't take long for the police to arrive and a few of us get arrested, although some of them manage to get away. So I get charged with affray and criminal damage. The Emergency Duty Team from social services came again and took me back to a family member.

I was getting used to being locked up and almost thought it was cool for it to be happening on a regular basis. It's not!

Three days later I left my family member's house heading for Mixenden. I was going to see my Mom at her house but when I get there she won't let me into the house and tells me to, 'Go away!' and to 'Go back...' to my family member's place.

I react badly to this and feel totally unwanted and unloved! Being told to go away by your own Mom is *never* very nice, especially when you're only 12 and struggling with your life First I get mad and start banging on the door, then I start kicking the door, I am feeling very angry now, almost consumed by my anger. *No one wants me, not even my own Mom.*

I get a large brick from the back garden wall and I walk up to the biggest front room window and put the brick straight through it. Then I just sit there waiting for the police to arrive and lock me up as that was what happened when I was naughty or making a cry for help.

It doesn't take long for the police to arrive and I get arrested and taken to the police station. This time I get bail with conditions: mainly not to go to my Mom's house? Now I would have to go and live with another family member with a 7 pm until 7 am curfew.

Over the next couple of months I stayed all over Halifax at different people's houses. I couldn't find a house it was back to the waste paper recycling bins in Netto's car park. Much of the time I was being caught "on the run" because I had breached my curfew, then it would be back to the courts in the morning and re-bailed by dinner time. This became a regular occurrence. But after a couple of months the courts remanded me to the care of the local authority and that meant leaving my family member's house to go to Skircoat Lodge Children's Home. This made me happy as Robert was in there and some of the boys from the bus incident lived there too.

14   I Need Help, Not Moving

So it's the 15th of March 1996 and I move to Skircoat Lodge Children's Home. I felt quite happy about this as my brother and some of my friends were there. I hung around with my brother and some of the older boys. On the first day there, we went out breaking phone boxes and it wasn't long before we were caught, arrested and charged with criminal damage. My first day there and I had already been charged with an offence.

The following day they moved me to foster parents in Southawram. I started thinking, "Why am I moving again? They're passing me on to someone else, nobody wants me! Am I that naughty?"

I didn't want to move, I liked it in Skircoat Lodge and I had only been there 24 hours. They were not giving me a chance to settle in anywhere, perhaps I'd been naughty but moving me on to somewhere else was not helping me. It felt as if they were just passing the problem on to somebody else.

I needed help not moving!

From the next day I was living in Southawram with a nice family and they spent time with me, took me places with them and I started feeling a part of their family quite quickly. I was settling down and staying out of trouble. I didn't breach my bail conditions whilst I was there, not once. Although this wasn't to last, my behaviour started to deteriorate rapidly when I found out I was moving again. I had to say "Bye" to the first real place where I was starting to see improvements in my behaviour.

Then, when I was moved, I felt like no-one had time for me. It seemed they just passed me on to member's of my family or the next foster parents without getting to the bottom of my issues and dealing with them.

On April 2 my social worker moved me to 193 Huddersfield Road. There were six other people there but they were all older than me. I didn't want to be there, I would much rather have just been back in Southawram with the nice foster parents. It wasn't as bad as I thought as it turned out, I got on with a girl in No. 193 who was a real support to me.

Robert was still staying at Skircoat Lodge and it was only a short, ten minute walk from where I was staying. So I started meeting him and other boys and this lead to me breaching my bail conditions again. I had started sleeping rough the odd night if I had to. Often I would stay at other children's homes, I would get sneaked in by my brother or other friends at various places.

I did it for five nights in a row at one point and the magistrates had finally had enough of seeing me so they said I was not to go back to No. 193. On April 13 they sent me back to Skircoat Lodge! I thought, "This is good, back with my brother and the other boys there." That's not what happened though. They moved me in and Robert out. He went to live in a children's home in Rastrick called Close Lea. That home was for older people in care who were getting ready to move out to their own place. So I stayed at Skircoat Lodge and just carried on with breaking my curfew almost daily and was still hanging around with the older boys who lived there.

Skircoat Lodge was a big building with another large one at the back called The Round House. Ironically it was round! We would spend our time in there sniffing gas, drinking, smoking both cigarettes and joints. The older boys would be entertaining girls of a similar age around 15-years-old. All the people in the home were starting to feel like family now and almost like brothers who stuck together. I could always talk to the other boys, they were all there for a reason but we never talked about it unless they wanted to. We were all in the same boat and that gave us a strong bond.

On May 2 they moved me to another children's home called Aloe Field View with children my own age. I didn't feel 12-years-old nearly 13. I felt like one of the older boys not like the kids there who were eight, nine, ten, eleven or 12-years-ofage. "These are not my friends — my friends are in Skircoat Lodge."

On May 5 I went to meet some of the boys from Skircoat Lodge. We went to Manor Heath Park, started drinking cider and got steaming. Then when we were really drunk we went walking around Manor Drive where my friend from school lived. We went back along near the park where three boys were waiting on the other side of the road. We crossed over and one of the older boys asks, "Where's your fucking money!" They hesitated not knowing what to do, so my friend punches one of the boys in the mouth knocking his tooth out. Then he took all their money off them. I didn't get a penny. I don't even know how much they got, I just got free cider and cigarettes.

We were arrested later that night for robbery. I admitted my part, watching. I would not name anybody else who was there though. That was their job. We were a bonded group. I got charged with robbery! So now I was on bail for aggravated TWOC, public order section 4, affray, criminal damage and robbery.

All this had happened in five months during which I was moved ten times plus. On average I would spend three nights a week in the cells for breach of curfew. I'd probably, by this point, been locked-up over 30 days and nights in the last five months. This didn't stop and I got moved from children's home to foster parents almost constantly.

On my 13th birthday I was back at Aloe Field View and I was keeping away from the other boys from Skircoat because of my bail conditions which were not to hang around with them or contact them. Plus Nev, who used to play football with Terry my Mom's ex-husband, was one of the staff there and he was trying his best to help me and I knew that! Nev was a cool man who would put extra time in for me during the time I was there and keeping out of trouble.

I was in court for sentencing on July 1, for all of the offences I'd committed. I was sentenced to a 12 months supervision order, and had to see a youth justice worker once or twice a week which was reduced as the order went on. Well that was it: no conditions, no curfew, no not seeing my friends anymore. All I had to do was see my youth offending team worker.

So now I'm 13-years-old going on 14 and have still not settled anywhere. I have just been moved from pillar to post by the local authority. I am not a happy boy like I should be at that age. They keep moving me because I'm disruptive, volatile but I am just a broken boy. The last year of my life has been awful and I'm trying to settle at Aloe Field View.

15 Meeting John

Since I've been on a supervision order I've been keeping out of trouble and out of Halifax, Manor Heath Park and the bus station. I've started back at Sowerby High School with help from Nev, youth justice, the home and my social workers. This excites me! I used to love school, now they've let me go back two days a week, but I'm not sure how long I will last as I was becoming naughty when I was last there. However, this was the first time I made a little progress. I had not been there for months but now I was with kids my own age and social services were trying to stabilise my chaotic offending and behaviour and nights in the police station. They say it's not good for my health to be locked up so much at such a young age. And what about all the moves I've had?

John Hodgson was a youth justice worker I had to work with twice a week. I like John, he is about 60-years-old. He takes me places and builds trust with me, he isn't always asking questions and I respect him a lot! I don't respect many people, in fact I only respect my friends. I don't respect authority, mainly the police but also I don't respect the staff at the children's homes, it seems like they don't care. They're just there for the money, apart from Nev and a man called Arnie. I have more respect for my youth justice workers because they are trying to help me and that is more than anybody else is doing for me other than Nev. Most people just tell me what to do!

John is different, I never give John abuse — not ever — but I give it to almost everybody else. I go out with John one day and he's talking to me about school and he says if I can be good he will try and sort a trip to Pennine Trout Fishery. He knows I love fishing, I've told him about my fishing spots and my angling experiences. I talk about Sowerby Bridge and how I want to move back and live there. That's the only place I have happy memories of. John tells me he can take me fishing to all of my favourite fishing spots in Sowerby Bridge. I am over the moon about this, it's the only good news I've had in ages. John is the best and I'm not going to let him down! I want to go fishing so bad that I have to behave myself. If it's even possible for me?

I go to school and I find it difficult to get back into the life there, my own life has changed so much and been so hectic since I was last there. I've been moved so many times since, not only that but I've been convicted of a number of criminal offences as well. I've spent over 30 days in police custody. I've been on-the-run, missing, smoking cannabis, drinking cider. I've had fights. I'm not sure how long I will last in school and away from my other friends. I don't know how long, but I'm going to give it my best shot for John.

When I'm in school I try to behave and concentrate but it's too difficult, I'm going to struggle so bad. But I just think of the fishing and John taking me too my best spots. John takes me to play pool and snooker the first few weeks and then announces we can go to Sowerby Bridge fishing next week and to keep up my good behaviour. He's the only person that has said that to me, John sees the good in people, he's the best. This gives me another boost and keeps me in school longer. I'm not enjoying it like I use to, Wayne and me have grown apart because I haven't been in school or seen him. We do speak and are friends but he has got new friends now, although we will always be friends!! I stick it out for the love of fishing.

The day comes and I'm going fishing with John. I am up early and readying myself, I don't want to be late getting to the youth justice office where I will be meeting him. I have to get a bus from Aloe Field View to the bus station in Halifax town centre and walk up through town past the courts and to Trinity Place where the youth justice office is. When I get there I go in and tell the receptionist, 'I'm here to see John, I'm going fishing with him today." With an attitude! For some reason when I go to youth justice or to social services my attitude changes. I am worse with the police. I hate police officers: all they ever do is lock me up and rough me up with the odd slap or punch. How could I possibly like them? They're all the same! They don't have time for naughty kids who are in children's homes — I've rarely met a nice police officer.

The receptionist says, "That's brilliant Ben."

I don't mind this receptionist, she is speaking to me nicely and looks and sounds interested in what I have to say, not like some other receptionists, all head down and working hard. This receptionist is young and pretty. I drop the attitude with her and leave her alone.

John comes out of the back of reception and into where I am waiting for him.

"Morning," he says, as jolly and smiling as ever.

I say "Morning" back and we make for the door and then to his green Peugeot 306. We get in and on the seats are wicker-type bead covers so that the seats don't get dirty, they aren't comfy in any way, shape or form.

John is a careful driver. He never goes over the speed limit. Not that I haven't asked him to, because I do and I always get the same answer, "Let's just get ourselves there in *one* piece!" I respect that it's his car and he will drive the way he wants to drive. I've asked him the same thing when he's taken me to pool, also when he's taken me to snooker.

"Well I have a couple of fishing rods I found and some old bits of tackle I dug out of the garage," says John.

Now I'm even more excited because I was thinking, "How are we going to catch anything with no fishing rods."

As we are driving to Sowerby Bridge we go through King's Cross and then down through Pye Nest and finally into Sowerby Bridge. We go through the town and over the bridge on the River Calder and take a left after the arch onto Station Road and pull up at the side of the outdoor market.

I can't wait to see what's in the boot. I'm like a normal kid would be in a sweet shop. We get out of the green 306 and go to the back of the car, I'm waiting in anticipation for the boot to open. It does and there are the two rods and a box with the tackle in it. We gather them up, then make our way across the road and over a bit of rough ground then under the arch to the other side where the river opens up and there are some weirs for canoeing.

Just where I had kicked Roy in the river for a laugh that turned into a nightmare. It's nice here but I haven't fished in a while, or been here fishing. We walk a little further down river to where we are going to be fishing and put the rods and box down. We admire the scenery for a minute and the bridge and everything around it.

Then John tells me he doesn't know how to fish!

"Well, *I* will show you John," I say to him in a surprised voice. I thought he was going to be showing me some ways of fishing and sharing some of his experience with me. But that's not how it turned out.

I get the first fishing rod out of its cloth cover and as I'm doing this I notice it's much thicker than my cheap, blue rod. I get both pieces out and find it's a seven foot sea fishing rod! I laugh at John and then with him. I explain how I don't think this rod will be appropriate for the River Calder.

The fish there are only small, up to three pounds at the biggest, he would be able to pull me in and land me with that sea rod! Then we get the second rod out. This is better, it's certainly thinner and lighter than the first one. It's also a lot older and made of wood. Maybe he used to use this as a kid

and forgot about it, it's that old! I asked where he got them
from and he said he didn't know, they were just in his garage
at home, with no further explanation.

Now to the box of tackle. I open it and find a reel inside
that has thick line on the spool of about 30 lbs plus breaking
strain. That must be for the big sea fishing rod! The second
reel was older but had thinner line on the spool. The rest of
the box had a few hooks and weights in it, but no spinners or
floats. So we have one big sea fishing rod and reel that can't
be used on the river with a line that wouldn't go through the
hook eye anyway. We share the thin wooden rod and reel.
We put a few pound weights on the line and a hook and two
maggots, one red and one white. We sit just to the right of
the weir and cast in and hope that a trout takes the bait. It
doesn't take long and we are in to a nice brown trout. It puts
up a little fight, the current making it harder and then I land
the fish and I am filled with joy and proud to have caught
one in the presence of John.

Over the next few hours we must have caught over ten
brown trout! Over the next four or five months I kept going to
Sowerby Bridge with John, to different spots and even found
some new ones up and down the River Calder.

I managed to struggle on through school to this point but
then I got suspended for five days for pulling a moony at the
teacher, for a *laugh*, but the teacher didn't see it that way at
all. I was hanging around Aloe Field View during the days,
getting bored and mischievous.

It didn't take long for my behaviour to deteriorate, I was
being abusive to staff again and disrupting the unit. Plus I was
arguing and nearly fighting with other young people because
I was bored and would annoy them to the point where they
would break and react to me.

I got moved from Aloe Field View to another children's
home, I wasn't interested in moving and I couldn't settle there

either because my behaviour was spiralling out-of-control or disrupting things so that I would be moved again.

I was sick of being moved. Up until then and with John's help, I'd stayed out of trouble for over six months and had tried my hardest, it felt like they were now passing the problem on again instead of tackling my issues and finding out why I was behaving like this. So school decided I wasn't to be allowed back in after all, what with the unsettling moves. Surely someone could handle me or put some time in for me and try and see why I was so unsettled.

Just before my 14 birthday I started back hanging around with the older boys and my brother. Sometimes when he came into Halifax he stayed at Paul, his friend's house. Paul was a sound lad but with learning difficulties. He lived under a cycle shop at King's Cross in a pokey basement flat. I went there even when my brother wasn't visiting... I've stopped in the same children's homes as Paul when I was being moved about and he was a resident at several of them.

16   The Summer of '97

The summer of 1997 wasn't a time I particularly enjoyed. We started taking speed and sniffing glue and Damp Start, smoking a bit of cannabis and taking sleeping tablets obtained on prescription. I also started to regularly self-harm and I was to get abused physically off foster parents in Bolton.

In May they moved me to Southgate, a children's home in Wakefield. "Out of authority"—I didn't like this, not at all. I'd always been in Sowerby Bridge or Halifax and their surrounding areas. No other kid's home was willing to have me in Calderdale, as I was so out-of-control, disruptive and I unsettled whole children's homes with my chaotic behaviour. So they shipped me out of authority to let someone who didn't know me see if they could control my behaviour.

On the 1 May 1997 I moved to Southgate. When I got there the member of staff was friendly and greeted me but I wasn't in any mood for Mr. Nice Guy. I had been moved out of Calderdale and away from my friends and family. Plus my sister had had a baby to someone in Mixenden and she was still 15-years-old. I had been trying with my Mom but she didn't seem interested. Plus she has another new boyfriend. When I see her I just stand there and don't speak—I think, *"I have nothing but abuse and rage for you."*

My social worker does her paperwork or whatever they do when they go into the office—I've sat outside too many waiting to be showed to a new bedroom. She comes out with another member of staff and shows me to my new room at the top of the house, up three flights of steps. When we get inside she tries to talk with me. I tell her, "Go fuck yourself, I don't want to stay here you fucking bitch, I hate you!"

She turns and walks away and shuts the door behind her as she leaves. As soon as the door shuts I throw my bin liner of belongings at the door, and start to swear and curse and kick the chair over that's in the room. I follow her downstairs.

"You fucking bitch I hate you, I hate you, I hate you,"

She makes her way down, past the office then for the door and her car. She gets into it and by this time I'm outside full of rage and almost out-of-control, I pick up bricks and soil and throw it at her car and stand in front of it swearing at her. I move out of the way after I have thrown the bricks and dirt and head off back inside, while she is wheel-spinning to get away from me as fast as she can. Everybody stays out of my way. They must be wondering what this social worker has dropped off at their normally peaceful unit.

Over the next week the members of staff try to engage me in activities and to talk with them but I refuse. After just over a week at Southgate I've had enough and can't take it any more, away from my friends and family. I want to get back to Calderdale and see them. So I set off out of Southgate and get on the road and follow it until I see sign for Halifax. It didn't take long. But it's on the motorway!

I sit down for a minute and think about either turning round and going back to Southgate or walking on the motorway. I decide I am not going back to Southgate! I will be walking on the motorway, going the million miles home. I set off down the slip road and keep to the left of the hard shoulder until I get to the actual motorway lanes, then I walk on the grass bank at the side of the hard shoulder.

I was walking and trying not to look at the traffic as I didn't want people to see me sobbing. I was 20 minutes into my walk when an Omega police car pulled up with its lights on. The policeman jumped out with a high visibility vest on so that the traffic could see him; he then came over and asked what I was doing on the motorway.

"I'm walking home!"

He tells me not to be silly and to jump in the back of his patrol car, then checks on the Police National Computer to find out if I am wanted or missing. The check comes back that I'm a resident at Southgate so he asks the controller for their phone number. Then he rings Southgate and tells them he has me in the back of his car and that I've been walking on the motorway, trying to get back to Halifax! Also, "Ben is very distressed and upset."

They tell the police officer to bring me back. He drops me off and goes and speaks with the staff about his concerns. I head off to my room and wait for the staff to come up and tell me off. They didn't do this, or try to comfort me in a time when I really needed it.

On May 12 they moved me to South Lodge in Derbyshire not far from Bakewell. I'm happy when they tell me I'm moving again, I think I'm going back to Halifax but that wasn't what they had planned for me, no I'm moving to Derbyshire and it's an activity children's home on a three kids to three staff ratio. This was meant to keep me occupied and it did.

I loved South Lodge It's in the middle of nowhere and there are activities planned from nine till five every day, and at night too. But this was only for four weeks and then I would be moving again because you can only stay there a month as its too expensive for social services. Hopefully, after the four weeks I'd be going back to Calderdale to a placement that could help me and give me the support I needed.

So I enjoyed my time at South Lodge but I still wanted to be back in Calderdale. No matter how occupied they kept me it couldn't stop thinking about home. It did keep me out of trouble and from committing crimes and being before a court. We used to go abseiling, rock climbing, canoeing and hiking. There was always something to do. But my time ran out quickly and on the June 9, just over a week before my 14th birthday, my social worker rang up to tell me I'd be moving to Bolton the following day and going to foster parents. I hated this idea and I hated my social worker, I wanted to stay at South Lodge if I wasn't going back to Calderdale. She informed me that she would be picking me up at dinner time the following day to take me to Bolton.

I tell her, "Fuck off... I'm not moving!"

She puts the phone down without another word. I am upset and thinking about running off—but where do I go with no money and nowhere to stay and when I don't know the area because I'm 100 miles from home?!

June 10 comes and my social worker turns up, I go out the door past her and head for some fields, but one of the staff from South Lodge chases after me. I give him the run around for a while and then just sit down. The member of staff comes and talks too me and convinces me that the Bolton foster carers will be really nice people and will have lots of time for me and I'll be able to maintain my good behaviour. This was the only place that didn't kick me out or get me moved to another place and I respected that. I walked back with him to South Lodge and collected my belongings and said goodbye to all the staff and residents there that had been so good to me.

Then we got in my social workers car for the drive to Bolton and the *"really nice"* foster parents...

17 The Witch and Darren

The journey to Bolton started off with me begging to stay at South Lodge or to go back to Halifax but my social worker reiterated what the staff there had said: that the foster parents sound *lovely* and that they seem *really nice*. I still wanted to go back to Calderdale, so I became abusive and told her what I thought of her. Again!

We pull up in Bolton on an estate, it looks just like Mixenden. Rough. There are little gangs hanging around, all probably up to no good. We proceed into the garden and it has a small council-type fence round it and at the side of the house is a tricycle. We go into the house and a woman greets us, she has mucky blonde or bleached hair and looks like she smokes 60 a day. I don't like the look of her, it's not what I expected — someone clean-looking with a friendly face. I didn't want to be here!

My social worker introduced me and the woman said, "I'm Christine". Christine asked if I wanted a drink, I replied, "Yes please", to which she retaliated smartly, "The kitchen's in there, make us all one!" I didn't like this woman and I felt like the staff from South Lodge were lying to me and so was my social worker, just to get me here. What a way to make me feel welcome in their home, I don't think so…

I went and made the drinks. While I was in the kitchen I was thinking about how I just wanted to be in Calderdale. When I had made them I went back into the front room. Then the horrible women showed me to my room. In the bedroom was a bunk bed and little else, it was a tiny, cramped room with a small window. Plus there was another boy's stuff in there too. I asked if I'd be sharing.

"What do you think?" she says.

I reply, "Yes", but I'm thinking "*I don't like your attitude and I've only been here ten minutes!*"

Is this what the social worker knew? Were they putting me here because the foster parents were strict? I didn't know, but what I did know was that this was going to be the worst place I had ever stopped at, by far.

Christine heads back down the stairs, whilst I just sit on the bottom bunk thinking, "*This is a nightmare, I hate it already, I just want to go home!*"

The social worker shouts up to me that she's going now. I just ignore her, I want to tell her she's dumped me in a shithole with people I don't know for about the 20th time but I don't want to upset Christine, she's already not nice to me and scares me. I haven't even met her husband yet or any of the other people that stay in this house.

When my social worker leaves, Christine, the witch, tells me, "You will behave in my house! You will go to education when it's on! You will go to bed at eight o'clock! You will do chores! You will basically do whatever me and my husband Darren tell you to!" I hated her instantly, I hated it there, I hated my social worker even more than I already did and this was just my first day.

The evening comes and her husband is back. He's of big build with long dark greasy hair in a pony tail. He tells me he is 'Darren.' He doesn't seem interested and wants me out of the front room. He tells me to go play out. I don't know anyone, I'm miles from home and I've only been here a day.

"Okay," I replied.

I get the hint and leave and go wandering around feeling lonely and sorry for myself. I walk around for an hour but not going far from the house because of the gangs and in case I end up fighting or get beaten up. I'm scared, alone, frightened, and miles from my friends. I just want to be at home. But by this point I have no idea where home is anymore.

After a while I go back in to the Witch and Darren's house, my *foster parents.* I walk in and the witch introduces me to her two sons. I say "Hello" then go upstairs not wanting to spend a minute longer than I have to in this woman's presence. Her sons are around 18-years-old. When I get upstairs and go into my bedroom that I'll be sharing, there is a boy in my room around the same age as me.

I say, "Hello, I'm Ben."

He tells me that he is "John", in a Scouse accent.

After that we chat for hours and we are friends in the same place and same position apart from he's been here longer. He doesn't like living here either. I'm not surprised that he doesn't, after my first day here I hate it. He tells me that he stays out all day as we aren't allowed in the house during school time. He goes to the woods a short walk away or to a big pond and watches people fishing. Well I love the sound of this! We get kicked out at nine in the morning and we aren't allowed back in till 3.30 pm when school's finished. This is brilliant, I don't have to stay in here all of the days and nights, and better still I get to watch people fishing! That is the next best thing to fishing in my eyes.

I wake up the next morning early, ready myself and wait for Scouse to get up and both of us to leave the house. I don't speak to anybody else. Scouse wakes up at 8 am being hollered at by Darren.

"Get up!"

"*Nice* morning call … ," I think to myself!

Darren jumps out of bed and gets dressed in double-quick time. "Let's go," he says.

I follow behind him because I am nervous and scared a little and don't want to go in the room first. Scouse walks in and no one is there, then we head for the kitchen. Darren is there with a bunch of keys on a chain hanging at the side of the leg of his jeans. It also has a fishing bar, what you kill fish with, it's a brass one of about five inches long. I think he must go fishing!

Me and Scouse make for the door and go, we don't eat breakfast. I just shut the door and we are out of there and that makes me happy. These are the worst foster parents I have ever met and I knew this within ten minutes of meeting them. Darren didn't even ask where we were going or didn't say, "Don't be late" or anything.

As we are walking to the woods through the estate there is a building site, workers are there but they won't be later. I say to Scouse, "We can ride them dumper trucks." He's excited and we discuss going there when the workmen have gone home, but until then I tell him he can show me the woods and the big pond. I couldn't wait to see the pond! I'm hoping to see someone catch something.

We get to the woods after a ten minute walk, they are massive and peaceful and full of wildlife with birds tweeting and big, lush green trees. As we walk into them woods there is a small stream. I run down to it and get to the side of the bank and look into the clear, running water to see if I can see any fish, but I didn't see anything at all. Then we follow the stream up in the direction of the pond.

I liked the woods and I told Scouse he had found a good place to come and get away from everyone and everything. He agrees and tells me this is where he spends most of his time, thinking about his friends in Liverpool that he misses and wants to go visit. I tell him about my journey so far in care and we find out we have both been moved to lots of different children's homes and foster parents. We get to the pond and it is big like he told me it was. There are couple of older fishermen there.

I say to Scouse, "Let's go and see what they have caught!"

He agrees and we walk up to the first fisherman and I say, "You caught owt mate?"

He replies, "Some bream and perch."

We sit and talk to him for a bit until I get the feeling he wants us to move on. Then we go to the second fishermen and ask him the same question.

"Have you caught owt?"

But this fisherman isn't too friendly so we walk off and sit at a distance and watch him fish instead. We stay there all day watching both of them fishing, and climbing trees at the side of the pond until we are allowed to go back in the house.

When we got back it was later than the time we had to be in, but I didn't care, I didn't want to be there in the first place. Darren and the Witch were waiting for us to return as it was seven o'clock and we had missed our tea that they had cooked for us. They shouted at Scouse more than me, he should've known better he'd been here longer they tell him. Darren waits for the Witch to leave the room and then gets in our faces and tells us "Don't fuck with me!" By this time he has his fish killer off his chain and then he hits us both on the head with it, and walks off as if it never happened.

We look at each other as if to say, "Hurry up". We finish our tea quickly and go back out, we don't ask their permission, I didn't care what they might think, I hated it there anyway and maybe they would move me. When we get outside I say, "Fuck bedtime, I'm not going back there, who the fuck does he think he's hitting like that?" Scouse doesn't say much, he just nods agreeing. Then we remember about the dumper trucks on the building site. So we head off there and climb over the fence they had put up to stop people from going inside because it's dangerous.

That doesn't bother me and Scouse though, we climb over the fence and into the site, then head straight for the dumper trucks. I'd driven one once before when I lived at Skircoat Lodge Children's Home when they were building houses to the rear of it near the rugby pitch.

We get to a dumper truck and wind it up with the big key type thing to get it going. It starts and Scouse jumps on and we drive around the site for 20 minutes or so until our attention turns to the chicken huts where the workmen have their dinner. We park the dumper truck just as we had found it so no-one will ever know. Then we set about trying to break into the hut, anything but going back "home". We fail, so we mess about a bit more then decide to head back to the Witch and Darren's place — the bullies house.

When we get back to the house they are seriously pissed off and ask us, "Where the fuck have you been?" says Darren in an angry, looming voice. We lie and say that we have been in the woods. They tell us to get upstairs. We go to walk out of the room and boom another blow to the back of the head! It hurt but I didn't show it. I just walked off and through the front room as if it didn't even happen. John got the same.

When we was upstairs in our bedroom I felt my head, I had two lumps one slightly bigger than the other. Scouse had almost identical lumps on his head, too. I hated Darren more than Christine now — at least she didn't hit us! But she let him do it.

I said to Scouse, "I'm going to tell my social worker!"

He didn't say anything, he was more visibly upset than me. We didn't speak much that night, just both thinking of getting out of there.

In the end I didn't tell my social worker. I didn't think anybody would listen to me. I thought, "I'm naughty, I've been moved homes for disrupting them, no-one is going to care what happens to me, they placed me here so ultimately it's their fault for putting me with animals." We just got on with it and a couple of weeks passed and it was the same most days.

We would go to the woods, pond, dumper trucks, get hit on the head with Darren's metal bar, then a month passed and it was all the same apart from the dumper trucks had been put in a new part of the building site and fenced in after the workers had finished with them for the day.

It was good while it lasted though, or that's what we thought. On another day we went to a blue lagoon were people could swim. This one day we were getting a ride to the lagoon with a man a lot older than us in his red van. He had picked-up half-a-dozen of us from the estate, there was him and one other person in the front and five of us in the back. I sat at the left-hand side on the wheel arch bit and Scouse sat on the floor next to me.

We set off and had been driving for around ten minutes when someone said, "We're here now, we just have to turn right into the pub car park." As we sat waiting to turn there was a big bang behind me and Scouse. Someone had driven into us. A few people screamed and we quickly got out of the van to see what had happened. There was a man of around 55 laid there motionless with thick pools of blood around his head. It was horrific and it still haunts me now.

We were taken to hospital for checks. Scouse complained of some slight pain. I couldn't feel anything, I was just numb from the sight of the man's face and the blood all over the place. He only had a piss pot helmet with no front to guard his face. It shook me to the bone, the worst thing I had ever seen in my life. The foster parents came and picked us up but they were not supportive in any way.

I later found out that the man on the motor-bike had died from the injuries to his head. He had been drinking and was over the limit. Still, not a nice way to go!

A month went by and it was a nightmare at best. I hated it more and more each day. I was feeling down, depressed, and thinking life wasn't worth living if I had to stay there. Me and Scouse got talking and decided we had had enough of the abuse off Darren and we would run away and not come back—ever. We weren't sure how we were going to get anywhere, we had no money. We decided to head for Liverpool. We were going to go the next day and that was final. We were not prepared to stay there anymore to be hit on the head whenever Darren seemed to feel like it, or when we was late or we had been messing around or misbehaving or generally doing anything this monster didn't agree with.

We decided we would jump a train to Liverpool, and we did just that. We walked to Bolton Railway Station and got a train to Manchester Victoria and then another to Liverpool. When we arrived, we headed for Toxteth where Scouse lived, hung around with his friends and stayed at their houses for a couple of nights. I would tell them about my Nana and her being from Liverpool. We got on great and they were kind to me. They fed me, and let me stay with them.

After two days of been missing the police found us and took us to a police station in Liverpool. We had to wait for a social worker to pick us up and return us to Bolton. When he came and collected us he was kind and happy. But we got returned to Bolton and the horrible foster parents. When we were inside we were told to go straight to bed as it was late.

Darren didn't hit us that night because the social worker was downstairs talking with them both. So we could relax. Just a bit.

18   Running Home

I lasted a few more days and I had had enough, I couldn't take it anymore and felt suicidal. I was thinking of a way to get home. To Calderdale. It was easy: "I'll just go to Bolton Station and then to Manchester and back to Halifax." I did this but almost got caught on the journey hiding in the toilet, dodging the fare.

When I arrived I was over the moon to have made it, I felt I was back at home and there is no place like home to me! I was straight up to King's Cross to see Paul but when I got there he wasn't in. So I walked round and round and back to his basement flat. He was still there, so I walked to Manor Heath Park and sat there thinking, "I have £2 and no other money, no food and I aren't going back to Bolton no matter what and at no matter what cost."

It was getting dark now and I was getting more and more down as the time passed. Then I felt total depression, alone, I couldn't possibly have felt worse. So I came up with a plan in my head and I was sorted. I would go into the shop and buy some Paracetamol. "I'll take them all and I'll be gone to heaven or wherever it is you go to …".

So I went into the shop and said, "My Mom needs some Paracetamol—she has a banging headache!" He gave me them, 50 in the tub. They were cheap, so I bought some pop to drink them with. Perfect! Couldn't have gone better in my eyes, I didn't think they would serve them to me but they had.

I go back to the park, I don't cry, I've done too much of that in the past couple of years, I've had enough of everything and I'm not going back to Bolton. Bolton made Paracetamol taste nice.

I just kept putting three in mu mouth at a time and swallowing them with a sip of pop. They soon went down; I thought I would just die! But I didn't. I walked back to Paul's and this time he was in. I told him what I had done and he insisted we go straight to the hospital.

After a short while I agreed to go to Halifax Hospital and get checked out. When we arrived after walking there we went in and I told them my name and age, but I couldn't give an address as I didn't know it. The receptionist asked again.

"I've run off from Bolton," I told her.

She looked concerned and caring. After I finished speaking to her she told me to go straight through to the doctors! I did and it was awful. I had my stomach pumped out and felt ill afterwards. They kept me in hospital for three days and while I was there I eventually told them how unhappy I was and how Darren would hit us with a metal fish killer, and I also told them how much I didn't want to go back there. One of the nurses rang the police and my social worker to inform them of what I had told her.

A police lady and another police officer came with a social worker and asked me some questions about what I had told the nurse earlier. I answered all their questions. I was told I had to go to the Viper Unit in Elland, so that the police could question me again and film the interview. I agreed to this and they went away. They were all nice to me. These were the first police officers I have liked, but I suppose that this time we were meeting me under different circumstances.

The next morning comes and I'm being discharged from hospital but first we are going to Elland to film me in a room with social workers and police. All being extra nice to me. I explain what I told the nurses, policewomen and social worker.

When it had finished the social worker asked if I'd like to go back to my Mom's and have a go at staying there? I was edgy, I didn't want to go home, I resented my Mom, and she hadn't bothered with me. She had left us and look where I've been since then. God knows how many placements or how many times I'd been locked-up. But it was definitely better than Bolton, plus I was back in Halifax.

So when the questioning was over, I moved back to my Mom's. I couldn't wait to get out of the interview room.

19   Back With Mom

At first it was okay but it all went downhill after a few days, my sister had a small baby and Mom a new boyfriend. I didn't feel wanted or loved. No one told me they loved me or that everything would be okay.

So within a few days I was back hanging around with the older boys and Paul, back within the week in the circle of sniffing gas and taking speed. I wasn't sleeping or eating and I looked ill. On the nights I slept at my Mom's, she knew I was taking something and she was straight to the social worker to report it. It seemed like "any excuse" to get me out.

The social worker said she was looking for another placement and in the meantime not to be doing anything stupid, little did she know I already was, taking speed, sniffing gas and committing crimes to get the money to pay for them.

So I got arrested on July 17 for breach of the peace and criminal damage. My Mom refused to come to the police station — surprise, surprise — so the EDT[3] was called again.

---

3.   Emergency duty team, i.e. at social services.

20 Spiralling

I got interviewed and released on bail to return to the police station. My Mom wasn't prepared to have me back again so on July 18 I was put back in Cousin Lane. I hated Cousin Lane before, now I seemed to hate everyone and everything there. I was an angry young boy that just kept getting moved and no-one was helping me. They just kept moving me on to the next place. Cousin Lane was boring with not much to do and I never liked it since getting arrested and moved away from there. So I started going missing again and made it clear to my social worker I didn't want to be there and to move me again as soon as she could.

In the meantime I'd be out as much as I could be. I thought, "I will stay at my friend's flat until I get arrested again." This soon happened and I was charged with breach of the peace because I was abusive when I was found and because I didn't want to go back to Cousin Lane. So they moved me again in September to Dewsbury Structured Unit.

A social worker took me there from the police station and I didn't know it was going to be at all like it was. We got there, out of the car, walked to the door and rang the bell. A member of staff came, unlocked and let us in, then we turned left and through another door into a big open room with seating at the back, a pool table and a TV and a sitting area. The office was on the opposite side, to my right, with lots of windows.

Once in the office they did some paperwork and checked I didn't have anything on me or in my possession that would harm me or anybody else. Then they took me through another locked door and up some steps to where the rooms were; it looked like a cell with a bed and drawers inside. I didn't care where I was, I'd been moved that much, I was used to moving by now. I settled in quickly as the boys in the unit were similar to me, there for offending when they wasn't in the unit. I got on with them okay. But after a few days I got into a fight with another boy over a game of pool. We threw punches and he got me with a good one resulting in me hitting the corner of the wall with my head, knocking me out cold. I was taken to hospital with concussion. After I had been released from hospital I was moved again after just three days.

I couldn't believe it, I actually hadn't minded being at the structured unit and now I was moving to Victoria Road in Elland. By the time I got there I was down and feeling really low and with everything I had been through and was going through I was out-of-control again. I was disruptive and being abusive to staff and the other kids. I used to be so naughty and not listen to anybody, and my behaviour was spiralling further out-of-control and at a fast pace. One of the staff there took me to her farm where her parents lived and I played in the hay and messed about. It was great at the farm and I enjoyed it. I also respected her a lot for taking me there as she did not have to do that. But she could only do so much to help me.

Around the end of September I got up on the roof of Victoria Road and wouldn't move. This was a huge house and very tall but there was a fire escape with steps going up the side of the house. If you get on the metal framing you could reach the roof and that's exactly what I did. When I got up to the top of the house I started pulling slates off of the roof and throwing them down the 30 foot drop to the ground. The members of staff came outside to see what was going on and saw me up there. They demanded I come down!

"Fuck off," I told them and carried on throwing the slates regardless, my head really messed up. After a short time the police turned up.

"Get down!"

"Go fuck yourself—I am *not* coming down!"

I carry on throwing slates off the roof in the policeman's direction. He quickly moves out of the way and goes inside the building. I just carry on throwing them and the neighbours are out looking and thinking, "What's going on." I ignored them, but I didn't want to hurt them.

After a couple of hours I'd had enough on the roof and came down. I was arrested and taken to Halifax Police Station and charged with criminal damage. Victoria Road said they wouldn't be having me back so next day they returned me to Dewsbury Structured Unit.

I'm happy back there playing pool and mixing with other young offenders instead of kids and the lad I had a bust up with has gone. It doesn't take long for me to start acting-up in the structured unit, I have no respect for the staff apart from one lady called Josey. She was ace, a very decent women who helped and talked to me as much as she could. But I disrupted the unit so bad that they wanted me out of there.

In October I got moved back to Halifax and in with foster parents in Norland. Norland is a beautiful part of Calderdale and it looks over Sowerby Bridge from high-up in the fields. They were decent people and they tried really hard, especially the lady, but I was too far gone and she couldn't help me—I don't think anybody could at the time. I was back drinking with my brother and his friends, we were fighting with people when we were drunk and just generally out-of-control. I had no positive role model to look up to. So at the start of November I got moved again, back to No. 193 Huddersfield Road.

I am out-of-control, I'm angry, messed-up and I don't care for anyone or anything other than my friends. I'm sniffing Damp Start on a daily basis and hanging round near the train tracks nearby. I'm a mess, collapsing regularly from sniffing—I get admitted to the hospital one night because I have passed out afterwards.

Everyone was concerned but I didn't care. I put my TV through my bedroom window, I assaulted another resident there because he was awaiting charges of sexual assault! In kids' homes this is not accepted. I got arrested and charged for section 47 assault. Later, they let me go back to No. 193 and the boy is still here who I assaulted! I let it go for a day or so, but after a few days I decide I'm going to assault this boy again not just for being a sex offender but for grassing me up and getting me charged with assault.

I went into the front room and he was drawing, so I picked up one of his pens then stabbed it into his hand! He screamed and ran straight to the staff. Again I was arrested and taken to the police station and charged with assault. They weren't having me back again, so they returned me to the structured unit in Dewsbury.

They tell me I need to think about my behaviour, my attitude, my anger problems and my chaotic offending. It didn't mean nothing to me, I didn't respect them and over the next ten days I was a nightmare for them. I was getting restrained almost daily and I was completely out-of-control.

So soon they move me again to High Leas in Whittington, Manchester. I'm not sure what High Leas are supposed to do with me, no-one else can control my behaviour and they couldn't either. There was other young people there and one of the boys I got talking to self-harmed, so I was soon as well and I cut my wrist to see if it would hurt.

I didn't feel any pain, it just opened my wrist wide, and I felt numb. I had to have six stitches in it. Then another time I took 100 Paracetamol, I had to go to hospital feeling very sick and had to drink cup-after-cup of charcoal. This is one of the hardest things to drink, it's awful and it makes you violently sick and your poo black—I would not recommended taking the 100 Paracetamol.

I was going to be dead soon if I carried on! But I didn't care. I was at the bottom and this was just in the first few weeks of being there, but I got worse, I was angry and annoyed, depressed, this was all my life felt like, "I am never happy. I don't do normal stuff kids my age do, I don't play on computers. I am out roaming, I cannot settle anywhere, I don't get time, I just get moved."

Once I snapped at a member of staff and went and got a big knife out of the kitchen drawer and went to look for him with it. I found him and threatened him with the knife and then went to my room. When I got inside there was some beads but like a rope of them. I wrapped them around my neck repeatedly and tied them to the door, so that when they opened it it would strangle me to death! These were scary times for me, I was struggling with life and sooner or later I was going to be dead.

Before long the police were banging on my door.

I don't speak, I can't, the beads are too tight. They try opening my door and it strangles me but the officer sees me chocking and panics and then shouts, "He's got a fucking rope round his neck!" The door shuts and I hear footsteps down the stairs running fast, and then back up again. The door opens again and I am being choked but it doesn't last long because the officer cuts it away and quickly enters the room and unravels it from my neck.

I was arrested and taken to the police station in Manchester where I was stripped naked and given a paper suit. Then an officer sat outside my cell checking on me every couple of minutes to make sure I hadn't taken my own life. After a while they take me back to High Leas Children's Home, but within an hour, a week before Christmas, three men turn up and come to my room. They tell me they are taking me to Barton Moss Secure Unit in Eccles, near Salford.

21 Secured For Safety

A secure unit? I don't know what one of them is, my head is puzzled I am confused, plus my mental health was not too good. I go with the men. I sit in-between two of them in the back of the car then set off to my new *secure* home. We pull up outside the gate after going on a dirt track, then you come to Barton Moss on the right just before a bridge. We pull inside once the gates have been released and opened-up for us. We park and go in a door on the left, I'm showed to one of the five bed units.

I'm a state: my mental health is a mess, I've lost control, I'm angry, aggressive and just 14-years-old. They tell me I've been made the subject of an order for the secure move. The social workers have said I meet all the criteria and more for this, on welfare grounds so I don't hurt myself or anybody else. It's all new to me being totally locked-up and allowed out for cigarettes at certain times in a courtyard with high walls so you can't get out. You can only go out of your room if one of the staff lets you out and that is the only time you are breathing fresh air.

The other boys are there because they are dangerous, some are murderers and boys with serious issues like me that need resolving and unfortunately this is the only place for kids like us who no-one else can control. The boys I spoke to told me how there was a boy there who had killed a toddler! This disgusts me. I think, "I *must* be bad" if they're putting me with these kinds of people.

I didn't mix with many people and certainly not the child killer. I didn't really know much about his case it as it wasn't talked about in my circles, I hadn't watched much TV, what with my chaotic lifestyle, so at the time I didn't appreciate that what he had done had been all over the newspapers! But still the thought of being in the same place made me want to harm him. I'm sure other boys did as well, but we were young and watched over 24/7 unless we were in our rooms at night. The boys were between ten and 15-years-old, and all dangerous in their own way.

The education department was brilliant and I started to think, "Maybe this is were I *should* be, I seem to be settling down, I'm not as angry and they are talking to me about my problems (the first place to do this) and they have let me know I can talk to someone anytime." They were encouraging me to talk, which helped. They made me feel as comfortable as you can be in secure accommodation. I got to catch up on the education I had been missing and received certificates for English and Maths and some other subjects. I couldn't stay there long though because the court was demanding that I have a full psychological test carried out on me and they didn't want to keep me locked up any longer than I had to be as they knew the type of young people I was mixing with at this place.

In and amongst the secure order and other things, I was back in court to be sentenced to another supervision order and an intensive training order. Then back to Barton Moss on welfare grounds. They would be keeping me for another month and helping me, even though I didn't always like it. Looking back, being there probably saved my life.

I met Christopher Eccleston the actor near Christmas time when I was there, he came to the gym hall and handed us all a book. I got a batman book, signed to me with a few words in. We did an English test on one of his films, *Let Him Have It*.[4]

---

4.   About the notorious Craig and Bentley murder case. There are countless references on the internet.

22 One Last Chance

The 16 February 1998 comes and I'm on the move again. I'm going back to my Moms to give it yet another go. She visited me once when I was in Barton Moss, plus I'd chilled out a lot since being in secure and my behaviour was better and I felt more at ease. I moved back in with her and everything went well at first but it didn't take me long to slip back into the old routine of hanging round with my friends. We was out drinking and taking trips, purple pills shaped like love hearts, and some of the boys were taking heroin, smoking it off the tin foil.

We had no money so I started to tax people and taking theirs, and their coats sometimes. One day at the beginning of May we were in the bus station and fairly drunk, giving people abuse as they walked past. We went outside of Deep Pan Pizza, and then inside to take some pizzas without paying. I was hungry, it ended up in a big fight with staff from the shop and a customer, and I hit out at both of them. The police were called and arrived there in minutes. I was arrested for affray and thrown in the back of a police van. A minute passed by when the back door of the police van opened and in shoots some CS gas. Then it shuts again leaving me choking in the back: I couldn't breathe, I felt like I was going to die, my eyes were killing me, stinging, then I passed out and the next thing I remember is waking up at the police station.

My Mom doesn't want me back so they move me to Dewsbury Structured Unit again and I was there one day before I got moved again to a remand foster placement where I stayed for just over a month until I got sentenced again at court.

Over the next month I went fishing and was also taken to a caravan site with the foster parents which I really enjoyed. I know they had to speak with my social worker and also my youth offending worker to get permission. They thought I would be bad and cause trouble or problems for the foster parents while I was there. I didn't and had a great time but I knew I was at high risk of being put in a secure training centre or other secure place.

They were talking about somewhere called Medway, it was the first secure training centre in Britain and it seemed that I might get sentenced to go there. Medway is for the worst young offenders in the country under 15-years-of-age.

23   Medway

Court comes on June 22, I'm nervous with all the talk of Medway and that I would be the first person from Calderdale to be sent there. We go into Halifax Youth Court and wait in the long corridor to all the courtrooms on the right as you look down it. I'm kept waiting for a couple of hours, nipping out for the odd cigarette.

I knew a lot of the young people hanging around the courts. It was always the same old faces when you went to court, so I always had someone to talk to. Or I would be a pain in the backside for the security people who would patrol the corridors and the front door where the young people smoked.

My name gets called so I go into the courtroom feeling even more nervous and not knowing what to expect. In there is a social worker, a YOT[5] worker and Mrs. Bramble my solicitor. They spoke about the crime and said how I viciously attacked the two people at Deep Pan Pizza, punching them and resisting arrest.

The three serious looking judges retired from the courtroom and went into the back to decide what sentence to give me. Before they came back, two Group 4 officers came in and waited by the door.

"I must be getting locked-up — that's why they are here," I thought, "they've buzzed them knowing they are sentencing me to Medway."

The judges returned and sat down and then told me my sentence: six months in a secure training centre in Kent.

---

5.   Youth offending team.

One of the Group 4 officers handcuffs me to his arm and leads me down to the cells, down the elevator on the left. I had come up and down this way so many times for breach of my curfew and once when I came from Barton Moss Secure Unit.

Stewart who looks after the court cells takes the handcuffs off me and puts me in the youth cell to wait for Group 4 to take me to Medway. Stewart is a good man, he's never judged me and always treats me with respect and, in return, I respect him. I don't give him hassle. I take the sentence and deal with it over a horrid cup of tea. I don't drink tea! I like coffee, Stewart knew that and went to fetch me one because he was a good man and all the people I know who go through the court cells only have nice words to say about him, even though he is locking us up, he is a very decent man. That is respect!!!

I end up waiting all day for the Group 4 van to take me away, but they don't arrive in time and the courts are about to close for the day so they transfer me to the cells at Halifax Police Station to wait for them.

It's not like it was when I first got arrested. I'm hardened to the police station and don't care for the police, at most they can hit me or slap me about but I'm older now and can take their bullying when it happens. It gets late and dark that's all I know when they turn up. They search me then let me out to a little white van waiting outside—not one of those with all the little square plastic windows, but a private one with four seats in the back of it. Two Group 4 officers get in the back with me while the other one drives. As we set off one, them tells me we are going to Manchester to pick-up another young offender. We drive over to Manchester and will then have a six hour journey to Kent ahead of us.

No-one said anything apart from the Group 4 staff trying to talk to us, but neither of us talked back to them. We were going hundreds of miles from home and wouldn't return for three months—not like them, they would be going home when they had dropped us off, so excuse me for not sharing their enthusiasm, chatter and jokes.

But I did need a wee on the way. They had to ring their office and ask what to do. Was they allowed to take me for one? They got told to call at a police station, so we pulled up around three hours into our journey. Two police officers came out and watched the van while another went with me and one of Group 4 officers to the toilet, to make sure none of us escaped!

It took a few more hours and then we hit Medway Secure Training Centre. It is next to Cookham Wood Prison in Kent. We get shown through the gates and into the area where you get out of the van and the gate shuts behind you—and that's when reality hits … No going home now!

We got strip-searched before being split up and shown to our different units. When you walk out to go to your unit you there is the dinner hall that you can see through the windows to the left, then in front are eight units, four on each side, all with different names of places. The gym and education unit are at the furthest point of the circle of the secure training centre, with grass in the middle and a bench for the Group 4 first response teams.[6] They hang around in the middle of the units near the benches waiting for their beepers and then run to whichever unit they are needed in.

I get put in my unit and there are five cells that look like bedrooms but with doors that lock. There is a shower to the left as I walked into my room and a peep hole so the staff can see you if you're not in the main part of your cell. There are thick plastic windows set between the bars, so you have light can't open them. In the middle of the unit is a kitchen area and a living-room-type area, with windows looking out

---

6.   Group 4 has ceased to exist as such. Medway is now managed by G4S.

onto the green and the bench with the Group 4 first response team waiting for any trouble that happens.

Medway was a rough place with many young people who were prolific offenders in their local area, or who had committed a serious enough offence to be sent there. There were lads of 14-years of age and already fully-grown like men. I was a small lad, certainly not big up against most of the other young people there. There was a North-South divide but I didn't get involved in that. If I liked someone I would talk to them no matter where they were from.

I had one good friend there called Ruben and he was the proud father of twins. He was only 14! He was a hard lad from Slough in Berkshire. He was feared by most of the lads in Medway but was a diamond with me. He looked after me and we supported each other, spoke about our families and what we had done to get ourselves into Medway. He was a tree surgeon, or wanted to be one, I'm sure he will be when he's released. We became one, and that made us stronger, we looked out for each other, could both handle ourselves. We would also play board games, cards, just about anything to pass the time.

On the other hand, Medway was kicking-off all the time and all over the different units. The Group 4 people earned their money with all the running they did. But they used far too much force on young people there: they bent them in two, used nose restraints on them, pressed behind their ears and knelt on them with great force—far too much force. I joined in with all the kicking-off, most of the young people did, it was "someone" for us to hit out at. The place would get trashed or anything that could be trashed would be once someone kicked-off and this was a daily experience. Sometimes I'd kick-off on my own when I was angry and fed up but I got restrained and manhandled like a man would be, and put in all different kinds of restraint positions.

There was one particular officer with bleached blonde hair that looked like a bird had shit on it — he 'looked a twat'! He loved using force on young people and twisting them up, and doing restraints on them.

Sometimes three or four of them (trained I presume in restraint) who would use shields on us at the most inappropriate times, when there was no need. No need at all for it, but no-one could complain, but that's not how it works in these places. I even saw them laughing and smirking while they are restraining young people, like they were getting a buzz.

The education block, however, was impressive, not at all like what I have just described. It was all modern and had brilliant facilities, a gym and indoor football pitch with a shiny new wooden floor.

I wanted out of Medway so I asked my solicitor to appeal against my sentence and she advised me I'd most likely be out by the time an appeal came through. I waited in Medway and the weeks passed by until I received a letter saying that I'd won an appeal hearing on the September 18, my brother's birthday.

So I'm happy and over the moon thinking I will be out just over two weeks before my present release date — if I get released. Just a few weeks and I'll be going to Bradford Crown Court for my appeal. The time passes slowly, all the trouble is still going on and with fights all over the place in different units. The staff are not in control, or they don't seem to be, and I'll be happy when I'm out of here and heading back home to Calderdale. Kent is hundreds of miles from Calderdale and I was missing my friends and family, and the lad who I got taken to Medway with escaped over a metal fence (but was caught shortly afterwards). I'm not sure what's outside because it was dark when we arrived.

My time passes by and it's the day in Crown Court for my appeal. On the morning we set off early for Bradford accompanied by three Group 4 officers. It's then I realise I have forgotten to get Ruben's full name and address, so that if I get out I can write to him. I still don't know where he is.

We get to Bradford Crown Court and I'm put in a holding cell and wait until it's my turn to go up in front of the judge. The Group 4 staff that brought me mingle with the rest of the firm's people. There are so many of them — it's a busy court with lots of prisoners in and out and going past my cell window. Eventually, I get called up and am handcuffed to one of Group 4 staff and I led up a long corridor and into a courtroom. Inside is my youth offending worker, a barrister, my solicitor, the judge and the five Group 4 officers to guard me — a thin little boy. As soon as the judge started, he asked why on earth there was so many of them with me and they explained that three had come with me and two were from the court. He told three of them to leave saying, "Murderers don't get this treatment."

I thought, "I've just less than two weeks left of my sentence, so even if I don't get released I've had a good day out." My solicitor speaks and argues that I should be released and there's a discussion between the prosecutor and the judge before he retires into the back of the court to make his decision. I've been here before and it wasn't a good outcome. He returns after a few minutes and makes a big speech that I don't remember a word of. All I'm interested in is what is going to happen to me. So what I do remember is him telling me I would be released that day but would have to do more supervision. I smile and am led back down to the cells the same way we came apart from this time I wasn't handcuffed. I was to be set free immediately and got a feeling no drug can ever give — the sensation when you're going to be set free.

My youth offending worker comes round quickly for me and we sign a few bits of paper and collect what little property I have. Then we are out of there and into the fresh air. I had a cigarette in my property and I smoked it, it felt like a baseball bat round the head because I hadn't smoked in the three months I was in Medway which was strictly no smoking. Then the youth offending worker took me back to Halifax Youth Justice Office while they found somewhere for me to go. They had to search hard as by then I'd stayed with almost everyone in Calderdale!

After a few hours my YOT worker told me they had found some foster parents in Todmorden, so on September 18 I went to them. When I got there I went straight out the back door and headed for Halifax to meet up with the friends I hadn't seen since going to Medway.

24 Rock Bottom

Nothing had changed in Halifax. People were still drinking and taking drugs, mainly heroin. Speed was long gone as was sniffing Damp Start or gas. I resisted the heroin and just got drunk and smoked a lot of cigarettes. I didn't go back to the foster parents in Todmorden that night, or any night. I just stayed with my friends getting drunk most days and enjoying being free and not being told when to go to bed or get up.

After ten days they moved me to yet another foster parent's house close to town on Saville Park, close to my friends and town and Manor Heath and Skircoat Lodge and No. 193 Huddersfield Road. They are all in the same square mile. I didn't stay there much, I was out the door and back with my friends, I was missing all the time and had stopped resisting the heroin everyone else was taking ... I had joined in, having resisted for weeks saying I would never take that, not ever. But when you're with a group of friends that are taking something it makes it so much easier to give in and join them. One day I said, "Fuck it, let me try."

I had nothing to lose, pretty much as soon as I was released from Medway I was out drinking and staying out, going missing and sleeping rough the odd night and now I had started to chase the dragon off tin foil.

After the first time, I took heroin with the boys on a daily basis, then I started feeling like I needed it — I was becoming addicted. I was staying at my friends' flats or houses, those who had left the care system and been left to look after themselves in life. The flats and houses I stayed in were scruffy, smelly, a total mess — with drug paraphernalia everywhere.

I was taking it with my brother and friends and one day we got talking about how we were going to earn the money for more drugs?

By the back end of October we had no more money for our daily hit of heroin, and it was getting from bad to worse for some of the boys who had been on it longer. We decided we would have to rob people to pay for it. So we went out and robbed a couple of boys who were walking down the street, taking money from them both. Then we would ring a dealer and go to one of the flats on West Parade and smoke what we had between us, and then go back out and do the same to other victims, ring the dealer, go back, smoke it. This became our pattern of life from the first day on. We would just rob people to feed our habit.

We couldn't stay in Calderdale long robbing people or we would have been easily caught, so we got Day Riders and started travelling Yorkshire robbing people of their money. We would jump on a train and go to a different town and rob someone and keep doing this until we had enough money not to need to go back out that day. Then we returned to Halifax with the cash we had stolen off lads our own age or even men. At one point we began thinking we was untouchable, riding round Yorkshire, being hard to track. We didn't care; we only cared about getting that money for the heroin. It got that bad we were losing weight and sight of what we was doing; how violent we was becoming.

We always carried a hunting-knife between us, taking turns to keep it. On one of the days we were in Bradford and had just robbed someone and had jumped on the bus back to Halifax. There were two lads about 18-years-old, sat at the back being loud. They had been drinking and were being abusive as well. We all glanced at each other and knew from the look in our eyes we were going to rob them. Before you knew it the hunting-knife was out and we were robbing these two lads of everything. Our little gang had become ruthless and we didn't care what the lads or any of the passengers on the bus thought. They were drunk and they had grabbed our attention. We rifled their pockets, took their coats and threatened them.

They stood up to get off the bus but we didn't let them, they were staying with us now, coming to Halifax with us at knifepoint. We got off there and escorted them to the cash machine and made them withdraw money from their accounts. But even that wasn't enough for our ruthless, greedy gang; we kept them till ten o'clock in the evening and made them withdraw more money, then sent them home. Then we went on a drugs binge with the hundreds of pounds we had robbed them of. That's just one of the days in our crime spree.

After the drugs binge I wanted a shower and to get changed and have something sweet to eat. When I got back to the foster parents, they knew I was on drugs and wouldn't let me in their house and told me they were ringing my social worker and that I'd be moving...

On the 21 December 1998, I got moved back to a children's home — No. 193 again. I never stayed there, I was beyond being helped — not that I had been offered much help. Apart from moving me on, no-one did much for me. But by now, I didn't really care much about myself either, I had been through too much and heroin took the pain away. I was out all the time with my friends, they had become my family over the years and we just carried on robbing people and taking more drugs.

Eventually I got arrested as did the other lads separately. I had gone to my Mom's house, I'd not seen her in a while. My life was a mess. I needed a bath and a clean, safe, warm place. I was tired from the drug use and not eating or sleeping. I got cleaned up, lay on my old bed in my old bedroom, the one I use to share with Robert and nodded off. I was exhausted.

I wasn't asleep long and my Mom came and woke me up and told me, "The police are here!"

"How would they know I'm here?" I asked.

As I looked out of the window I could see them. I'd not been here in months. I knew something didn't ring true, I'd must have been grassed up by a girl my brother was seeing. She had been at the house, but she wasn't there now, so between my Mom and her they had rung the police and told them I was at my her house! As I looked out of the window there must have been 15 or 20 police officers, men and women, some in uniform, some CID.

My Mom let them in and I was arrested for about 15 street robberies and the robbery at knifepoint on the bus. I got handcuffed by one of the officers and led to a waiting van. I looked down the road and there must have been ten police vehicles! I was taken to Halifax Police Station and put in a cell to wait for the appropriate adult to come, for my rights. There was no rush as far as the police were concerned, I was going to be staying in custody for a while so they could sort out all the offences.

Time went by and someone from EDT came and stayed for my rights, then they stayed on for my interview. I was questioned about the robbery on the bus and lots of other, some we had done and some we hadn't. It felt like they were trying to pin everything that was unsolved on us! I denied all knowledge of everything, The interview went on for some time as they tried to make me admit things, but I couldn't do that, these were my friends they were talking about. Then I was put back in my cell, kept there overnight and interviewed again the next day when they had more evidence. The questioning always started with the same questions and I just said "No comment" throughout the interview. I had had enough of staring at the four walls and being asked the same questions repeatedly. Prison seemed like it would be better than the two nights I'd spent in police custody.

The interview finished and I was put back in my cell all day and night and then they said I was to be bailed to return to the police station. I told the police nothing and mentioned no names; as far as I was concerned at that point I hadn't done any robberies and I didn't know what they were talking about. And I certainly wasn't going to drop my mates in it or *grass* them up.

After my release from police custody I started to cut down on the heroin. I had no way to feed the habit after borrowing money to the point where I couldn't get anymore. Heroin is hard to kick but I was determined to get off it. I was worried now and what I had done had started to sink in. I knew I would be going to prison if I was charged with the robberies. I stayed on at my Mom's house but I did ask if she had grassed me up, to which she replied, "No!"

I didn't want to believe she had but I knew she must have had a part in the police coming round; it was too much of a coincidence. I decided to sit in front of her fire and come off the heroin. I'd not been on it as long as some of my other friends and I didn't inject it so my rattle wasn't as bad! I was glad I hadn't gone too far with it. If some of the lads I was hanging around with didn't have heroin for a day they were in a far worse state than, but they injected and needed it more than I did.

I was determined to stop committing robberies as well. I wanted to be clean and wished I hadn't robbed all the people I had with my friends. I felt bad for those we had hurt and I knew I deserved to be sent to prison. I didn't grow up thinking, "I want to rob people," it just happened and I could not control it once it had started.

My life had been so hectic and unsettling. I had almost lost sight of the life I had in Sowerby Bridge and how happy

I was then. Life couldn't have been worse since leaving there. I knew I'm going to a young offender institution when next sentenced.

In the meantime I was sorting myself out: I was weak, looking scruffy, with rotting teeth and so thin, like I was bulimic, and I knew this wasn't good. I'd always been physically fit and played football, rugby or gone running—I had never felt like this, some of the worst days of my young life.

After a week my Mom said I'd to go back to the children's home now. I did but my bed had been taken by another young person in need of it. I was sent to more yet another set of foster parents.

I was still weak and didn't have much fight left, all the past seemed to catch up with me—all I had done for years was fight everybody! Fight the system, fight the police, fight anybody. I just went to foster parents and after that to my Mom's again, after she had moved out of Halifax.

The day comes when I have to answer bail. It's April time now: I go to answer it in a lot better condition than just over a month ago when I was last in custody. I had psyched myself up ready to go to prison. I met my solicitor and she told me I might be remanded in custody at court next day if was charged. We went into the custody area and my appropriate adult was there as well as DC Mawson—the smug police officer that's dealing with the case. When I get to the desk they tell me I'm getting charged with eight robberies and false imprisonment. I felt broken, gutted to say the least. I was kept for court and then remanded in custody to a young offender institution.

Prison wasn't the best place in the world, but when I got there and was shown to my wing I knew about five or six other lads who were there. I had lived with them at some point or another when I was being moved all over the place to different children's homes, foster parents and the structured unit — there was also a boy from Medway, so he didn't learn from that experience either. I had it pretty easy that way. But in my cell for the first night I cried and felt suicidal but I didn't want to self-harm, I had grown out of that and it wasn't an option.

I was big enough to commit the crimes so I was big enough to take the sentence when they gave it to me. I didn't like the fact that I was looking at two to three years in prison but I had been locked up before in Medway and Barton Moss, so I knew I would survive in prison and I did. I was later let out of remand and went to my Mom's new house. My brother and sister lived there outside of Halifax too. Even my Dad came and visited; he had broken up with his wife and was sniffing around.

Thirteen days after my release on bail in June 1999, I was up for sentencing at Bradford Crown Court. I got up early that morning, in fact I hardly slept at all the night before worrying about the sentence. I packed all my stuff into a big bag as I knew I wasn't coming home. I was looking at two to three years in a young offender institution. I was sure I'd be getting a custodial sentence and had got used to the fact. I'd thought about it over the two months I was on remand and got used to the idea.

When I was inside I was starting to stabilise my anger problems and drug problems. My head and mental health was picking up also. I even got my teeth sorted out a bit and my general hygiene. Don't get me wrong, I liked it being out but I knew I was getting better inside and youth custody was the only place since Barton Moss and Medway Secure Training Centre where I'd seen improvements in my behaviour and mental health.

Once my stuff was packed, I got changed into my blue jumper and trousers. Most of my clothes were hand-me-downs or other boy's clothes they'd left at children's homes. I was moved so much I lost all of my own clothes and possessions Then I went and brushed my teeth and prepared myself for court. After I was ready, I went and said my goodbyes to my sister and nephew and brother and, finally, my Mom.

25   The Only Way Is Up

I am nervous about going to court! I think about running away and not going there at all. Then I think there is no point in running-off, that I will only get a bigger sentence when I get caught.

I head off to court and meet with my youth offending team officer. When I get there he is waiting for me and tries to comfort me, but I know I am going to prison no matter what he says. I regret doing what I did to the people we robbed but that was not going to save me from a custodial sentence today, all I could do was sort my life out when I got out.

We, me and the other boys, all have the same solicitor so we know what everyone is saying. She tells me that the prosecution want to make a plea bargain . . . I listen and she tells me if we plead guilty to some of the offences then they will drop the others and just deal with the most serious ones. I agree with what she says. Then I go back into the waiting area outside the courtroom and wait to be called into court. It is one of the most awful waits I've ever had!; knowing I am going to prison no matter how sorry I am or how much I am trying to change my life.

I and one of the other youths get called in to the courtroom and two are on custodial remand so when we get inside they are already as they have come up with Group 4 officers from the cells. We all say, "Hi" but this is not the place for a chat, this is a serious matter and if I am honest I am shitting myself. Court starts after the judge enters.

The prosecutor outlines the case and then our barrister stands up and tells the judge we will all be pleading guilty to

the remaining three offences of robbery and the false imprisonment. The judge tells us that we have terrorised people,
assaulted them, taken their possessions and that this is a grave
crime! Then he sentenced us.

Matthew got two years eight months as he was 18-years-
old. I got 16 months. The other two got 12 months apiece.

Then the judge told us it could have been a lot longer, but
that he had taken our guilty pleas into consideration. I knew
I was going to YOI anyway but the feeling I got when sentence was given out was awful, I could of passed out with all
the emotions running through my head

We were led down the steps in handcuffs, said our goodbyes
and that we would write to each other. Matthew and I got put
in a holding cell together. I told him this was it for me and I
wouldn't be going back to prison again or be committing any
offences when I got released. I wanted a new life away from
heroin and hurting people, I had done enough of that. I was
not proud of it. I was just surviving with no-one to look up
to, but ultimately it was my fault. No-one made me do those
offences, I could take the sentence and learn from my mistakes
during the long nights in YOI thinking about what I did to
the victims. This was one of the last times I would see him.

They took me to Weatherby Young Offender Institution
with another boy. When we got there it was the same routine.
I got strip-searched and given a blue uniform.

I got to go to Collingwood Wing. As soon as I got there I
met a lad called Ryan who I had grown up with and who had
been in some of the same children's homes as me. Ryan was
a good lad. He had his problems like me, as did most of the
lads there. He was established on the wing and I respected
him as well. I had known him for a few years and we was
real mates not just prison mates. He helped me through the
first part of my sentence and we would chill out together on
association, and play pool with each other.

In my cell I felt down at first. I had lots of emotions, getting my head around the sentence, but I also appreciated that I could have got a much longer one. I knew I had to get used to the empty cell and make this my home for the next six months. I knew from that point on that I was definitely never coming back there. I didn't want to be in-and-out of prison for my entire life, or taking heroin or sniffing anything like that. There has to be a better life than drugs and crime.

If I'm honest, when I was inside I enjoyed it in a weird kind of way. I was playing football again, and I started weights to build my strength back up. One of my favourite times was playing rugby with a medicine ball on the shining wooden floor in the gym. Like me, most of lads would get big burns from the floor and it was a rough game! Picture 20 boys on each side and the medicine ball gets thrown in, it's Bedlam, big hits going in all over the place, and some boys just wanted to inflict damage on other lads and let their aggression out.

I was also doing education, something I now only did when I was locked-up. I enjoyed it and was even doing art at evening class. Plus you get three meals a day, again something I was not used to on the outside. My hectic lifestyle on the outside didn't allow me to eat at normal times and some days I wouldn't eat at all. I got regular clean clothes and a shower in prison as well. I knew I had to get my head down and keep doing my education.

I also played football and got a job in the gardens, mowing the lawn and picking tomatoes out of the greenhouses. Anything to better myself and keep me occupied so that my sentence would pass quickly.

I'd be out for 2000, by the New Year, and I would sit in my cell thinking about this and about staying out of trouble and away from drugs and crime. There was a better way than prison and drugs and everything that goes with them.

I hear my brother is taking heroin with his girlfriend (who I still think grassed me up at my Mom's house). He's supposed to be a right old mess … and looks poorly, I don't want to be sick like Robert and many of my friends. I want holidays and to start living, not just surviving, existing, I want a new life, maybe even a new destination, who knows? One thing I do know is that I am never coming back here. Over the next few months this feeling was getting stronger and stronger.

"I'm not taking drugs! I'm not going to commit crime! I'm certainly not coming back here again."

I was also hearing of friends overdosing on heroin and dying from it, or hanging themselves because they couldn't handle what life was throwing at them. Life can be cruel to some people, like lots of the people in my circle. Some of them had been in care like me and had had horrid experiences of the care system before moving onto drugs, prison and, in some cases, death. Its just a revolving door, going round and round with no proper intervention, no-one helping us, just locking us up. Most of my friends don't have anywhere to go when they get out and ultimately commit crime and end up taking drugs and end up back in prison. I must have seen a lot of people get out and within a month or two they would be back inside with another sentence.

I didn't want to be part of this anymore. I was doing well in education and passed a couple of exams and I was even getting better at art. I made a kitchen cabinet out of wood for my youth offending worker, Bill, which I was really proud of. I was fitter and more positive-minded. I was also in a lot better frame of mind and looking healthy, but many people do when they leave prison. It's having the will power and determination to stay clean and not commit crime when you get out that matters.

My release date is fast approaching and I don't have long to go, I'm getting all excited about it and what I am going to do when the time comes. The hours are feeling like days and the days like weeks. I have been counting down the days on my calendar.

All I know as the time approaches is, "No more crime and drugs for me, I've had enough of the system and can't wait to get out of here and begin a new life."

26   Never, Ever Give Up

When I was released I moved back in with my Mom and her boyfriend who had by that time returned to Sowerby Bridge, to Sowerby New Road in fact where I used to go to school and enjoyed the best days of my life. Things had changed. I was more of an adult than a kid. I had grown up in prison. I stopped hanging round with the friends I committed crime with and took drugs with and moved on to a new chapter in my life.

I watched the millennium come in with the sky full of fireworks, there wasn't a space in it, a beautiful sight that I will never forget. I got on to a course called Project Challenge, and that really *was* a challenge. We did mountain climbing, improvised rescues, first aid, navigation and skiing. If you made it to the end of the course you got to go on a two-weeks expedition abroad to put into practice what had been learned. We trained for nearly six months and I made it to the end and was repaid with a walk on the Alta Via 1 in Italy.[7] It had some of the best views I've ever seen, unbelievable sights I'll never forget. It was one of the best experiences of my life.

I went to Glastonbury 2000 when Travis headlined, I also saw Macy Grey there and other top bands and artists. I met one of the best friends you could wish for but sadly he had to go back to South Africa as his visa had run out. I hope to visit him soon. I will never forget the close bond we had and still have, he is called Graham Poultney.

---

7.   A 150 km long footpath (also known as the Dolomite High Route 1) running through some of the best scenery in the Dolomites.

It has not always been an easy ride since giving up crime and drugs. I have suffered with severe depression, anger problems down to loss, not grieving and bottling things up instead of talking to people and letting them help me. I have been unlucky with my health as well, I had three major shoulder operations, a mastectomy and an open hernia operation that took 16 staples. *The key is to never, ever give up.* I got that tattooed on my back to remind me when I feel low!

So where am I now? I'm nearly 30-years-old and have never been back to prison, taken heroin or sniffed glue. I believe everyone can change: you just have to want to do it enough. And, if you have hit rock bottom, the only way is back up again! I have new friends now, but I'll always be friends with people I knew in my past life. Some of them have also moved on in their lives and are doing well now, including Ryan.

I have a son called Jack who is amazing. He was born on the 28 November 2002 at 11.23 am and weighed 7lb 3oz. I wrote this book to give to Jack when he's old enough to understand the life I've had. He's ten now, not much older than I was at the start of my story, and even if I say it myself I'm doing a brilliant job with him! If I had chosen drugs and crime I wouldn't have been here now, I'd have been dead or in prison and I wouldn't have my beautiful son.

The same day as he was born, Matthew, who I got sent to Weatherby Young Offender Institution with, died; just hours after Jack's birth. Matthew was the first person I told that I was never getting into trouble again. He overdosed on heroin. I found it hard, Jack being born on the same day that he was left to die. Matthew was a good, good friend and we shared some good and bad experiences together. He is in a better place now, I hope.

Wayne is still in Sowerby Bridge; he finished school and originally joined the army but has since left. He is happy, with a family of his own. I see him driving around and we wave and smile. Good memories. I have also spoken to him on the phone and told him about this book!

John Hodgson my youth justice worker I met recently too and had a coffee with him. He is still a "top man" who I have enormous respect for. Roy is still around but I don't see him. Robbie I did see recently at the railway station with his dad, he looks well and it was nice to bump into him again.

My sister Natalie has three wonderful kids, a job working with people with adult learning difficulties, a house and a mortgage. Robert is still battling drug misuse and has had two strokes in the last 12 months.

Life is full of challenges and choices, you just have to face up to them, try to make the right ones. Once I heard that Matthew had died, at that moment I vowed to never let Jack go through what I had been through, or Matthew. I know I have to love Jack and protect him and be there for him no matter what! Having him and losing Matthew confirmed to me that I will never go back to my former life.

I want to help as many other young people as I can to get out of that kind of life. I want them to get listened to as well. I began with User Voice[8] shadowing a talented national youth co-ordinator called Cordelle. Mark Johnson is the founder of User Voice and a big inspiration: a man who has lived life and written about it in a book called *Wasted*. Another lady there who helped me when I was starting out to work with young people is Anne-Marie. I have left User Voice now to do my own motivational talks to inspire young people in care and young ex-offenders. I want to go out there and make a difference; to tell them no matter how bad a start in life they've had, they can always have a bright future with some hard work and willpower. I want to use my own negative past to make their experiences more positive. I also want to raise awareness for

---

8. See www.uservoice.org

young people in the care system and to see what we can do to make life a more positive experience for them.

I am also on the Advisory Board of Spark Inside.[9] It's a life coaching charity that helps young people when they leave custody. I've been through this so my aim is to help as many young people as possible; and hopefully inspire them not to commit offences or take drugs. "Ex-offenders are people too!"

Nowadays I live in a nice place looking down on Sowerby Bridge and this makes me happy. I've fished at Hill Top Dam a few times too, but it's all overgrown and there is hardly anything to catch in there anymore. Not like it was when I was younger, it needs some TLC, the trees and grass cutting back and a general clear-out. One of my other dreams is to get the dam clean and fishable again. It's the ideal place for a project with young people!

---

9.   See www.sparkinside.org

Index

So You Think You Know Me?
by Allan Weaver
Foreword by Mike Nellis and Fergus McNeill

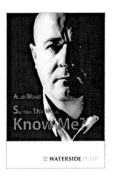

The autobiography of an ex-offender and twice-times inmate of Barlinnie Prison, now a social work team-leader in his native Scotland. As a local hard case, author Allan Weaver took no prisoners. Neither does he in this compelling work in which he tells of a life of violent episodes and his chaotic early life. 'I thoroughly recommend this book': *Probation Journal*

Paperback ISBN 978-1-904380-45-0 | 224 pages | 2008

Why Did You Do It?:
Explanations for Offending by Young Offenders in Their Own Words
by Jackie Worrall
Foreword by Paul McDowell

The voices of young offenders—the real life stories behind the worrying and sometimes tragic lives of those who get into trouble with the law. Setting these within the context of descriptions of youth justice policy, Jackie Worrall conveys to her readers an understanding of how and why young people become offenders going far beyond that to be gleaned from everyday rhetoric and theory. 'Having worked with offenders for decades, Jackie Worrall's experience and knowledge is unparalleled': *Paul McDowell, CEO, Nacro*

Paperback ISBN 978-1-904380-74-0 | 176 pages | 2012

Lightning Source UK Ltd.
Milton Keynes UK
UKOW04f0131210914

238915UK00006B/46/P